OVER THE GREEN HILL

A German Jewish Memoir
1913–1943

by
LOTTE STRAUSS

Fordham University Press
New York
1999

Library of Congress Cataloging-in-Publication Data

Strauss, Lotte.
[Ühber den grünen Hügel. English]
Over the green hill : a German Jewish memoir, 1913–1943 / by Lotte Strauss.
p.   cm.
ISBN 0-8232-1919-4
1.–Strauss, Lotte.   2.–Jews—Germany—Berlin Biography.
3. Holocaust, Jewish (1939–1945)—Germany—Berlin Personal
narratives.   4.–Berlin (Germany) Biography.   I.–Title.
DS135.G5S7713   1999
943'.155004924'0092—dc21
[B]   99-33711
CIP

Printed in the United States of America

In memory of

Louis and Johanna Schloss
my father and mother

Ludwig and Ilse Schöneberg
my uncle and aunt

may eternal life be with them

FOR THE DEAD AND THE LIVING
WE MUST BEAR WITNESS

CONTENTS

PREFACE

This book was begun as a letter to my daughter in 1993. I consider it natural that a young child should be protected from stories of horror that she cannot absorb and that might cause unnecessary anxieties. Anyhow, as Jane grew older and lived in our German Jewish environment, she heard enough and understood what had happened: she always knew of our and her Jewish identities.

Herbert and I had married in Bern, Switzerland, in 1944 and had come to the United States in 1946. Janie (as she came to be called) was born six weeks after our arrival in New York. I named her after my mother—Johanna. We had a happy and fulfilled life and were absorbed with bringing up Janie in our new freedom. We had to overcome the initial difficulties of immigration in the postwar world when U.S. soldiers returned home to begin families and start new careers. Living space was hard to find. At the beginning, we lived in genteel poverty, dictated in part by the poor salary a beginning college teacher earned at the time, and in part by Herbert's refusal to accept the assistance of a Jewish welfare organization. He wanted to do it all by himself. On a seasonal schedule, I worked in a millinery shop to augment our income.

At one point, close friends of ours, Harold and Lenore Gray, put me in touch with the League of Women Voters of New York State, which maintained an office in New York City. Harold Gray was the chairman of the academic department of the Juilliard School of Music where Herbert taught at the time. It was a stroke of good luck for us, because the Grays adopted our small family as theirs. Their informality and humanity opened up an aspect of American life we had not known before. With them our enthusiasm for American civility really began. I bear them a lasting debt of gratitude.

The LWV—before any other feminist organization—fought for civil rights and the expansion of equality for all members of society which I had missed in Germany and also in Switzerland, and so I found a new home in the League's pragmatic liberalism. From 1960 on, Herbert taught history at The City College of New York on a tenured professorial line.

In 1982, I went with Herbert to Berlin, when he accepted an assignment at the Technische Universität (Technical University) of Berlin to found a Center for Research on Antisemitism. We stayed in Berlin until 1990. At first, these eight years were a harrowing time for me, but, through the work done at the Center, I learned to see our own personal story more in context with overall history; thus, I gained confidence to express in words what had only been pictures in my mind I carried around with me for such a long, long time.

Finally, my hesitation to explain to my family and friends the total lawlessness and deprivation we had experienced vanished when we visited the Holocaust Memorial Museum in Washington on its opening day in 1991. Its motto—cut in stone—says, "For the dead *and* the living we must bear witness."

In writing this book I obeyed my own impulses to save the past from oblivion, but I would not have begun without the encouragement of my friends over the years. I feel grateful for their persistent interest.

Among them I owe special gratitude to the following: friends in the German American Women's Club in Berlin, especially to Dorothea von Hammerstein. They offered me a bridge between the cultures. In New York, our friend Arthur Tiedemann encouraged me in conversations over many months and shared his interest in and knowledge of contemporary history. Maria and Norman Marcus, New York, deeply empathized with my history and wanted to see it in print. Daphne Dennis helped me to produce a clear text through a series of revisions. Dr. Mary Beatrice Schulte, of Fordham University Press, edited the manuscript with personal involvement and understanding. Finally, the book would not exist without the advice of my husband. He knows how much my writing owes to him, so I will say only, "Thank you, Herbert."

Over the Green Hill

1

Childhood:
Salzkotten and Wolfenbüttel
1913–1920

December 19, 1993

Dear Janie,

Over the years, I have often toyed with the idea of writing down our history as Jews in Germany during the Nazi years and telling you of the background of the extraordinary time we lived through. It was and is my fear that doing so would recall deep emotions that are better avoided if one wants to lead a normal life, being loving and cheerful with one's family and pursuing daily tasks and interests. It might prove too difficult. I also have had a strong urge to leave a record of a time of horrors and genocide of such proportion that they are impossible to forget. This ever-widening net of murder during World War II engulfed Germany, where all of us—family, friends, and acquaintances—were entrapped. We two, Herbert and I, were able to free ourselves. My parents, Herbert's father, and our circle were not. The memory of all these innocent people being murdered at times overwhelms me. It can happen on walks in Riverside Park or on the Riederalp, or while I am washing dishes, peeling potatoes, or at any moment, when I get this stony feeling—"How could this have happened?" or "Why?" There is no explanation or understanding possible. I have a deep feeling of sadness and, at the same time, a closeness to these happenings and to the fate of the people with whom I most identified. Often I see a picture in my mind of hundreds of people marching up a green hill; they come in groups, singly or in pairs, talking to each other, holding each other's hands. After they reach the top of the hill, they walk right on down the other side without turning their heads: first their bodies disappear, then their heads. They are gone! I know that I will never see them again.

How can I write about this time, about my escape, about being alive, without mentioning all those who perished? My parents, aunts, uncles, friends, and almost everybody I knew: all those who disappeared behind the wall of silence. My emotions are linked to them. Therefore, my story will not be objective, because my feelings are not neutral, and I will not attempt to make them so. In telling my story, I will try to contrast the lives that Jews had in Germany, during a time when they were, at least, tolerated, with the changing times I lived through, when nearly all of them became innocent victims. Telling this story has—with time—become an obligation.

I was born and raised in Wolfenbüttel in Northern Germany. My parents were Louis and Johanna Schloss: they were Jewish. My mother's maiden name was Johanna Bildesheim. She came from a small town in Westphalia. My birthday was August 2, 1913, which became an historic date one year later: the day "when the lights went out all over Europe." World War I had begun, bringing on the turbulence that changed the fate of the European continent. The first year of my life, however, fell into the peaceful times that became known as "La Belle Époque." My parents named me Lotte, after the character in *The Sorrows of Young Werther*, reflecting the great admiration German Jews had for the works of Johann Wolfgang Goethe. Two years later, my brother, Helmut, was born, and our small family was complete. We had a large extended family, though, made up of my grandfather, the patriarch of the family, my grandmother, numerous uncles and aunts, and many cousins and second cousins.

Because Jews were in general excluded from Christian social circles, Jewish social life was limited mostly to the Jewish family. Visiting one another was the custom, as often as vacations or off-business time allowed, with frequent, lively comings-and-goings at our house. As a young girl, I felt attracted to the visitors. Their animated conversation, even when I did not understand it fully, raised my curiosity. I asked many questions. I guess I must have been a precocious child, which had advantages and disadvantages for me, depending on the approval or disapproval of the individual adult. But I do not recall that I often felt rejected.

I did not know then that this enjoyable family life was needed as a counterpart to the suppression the Jews had experienced for a long time in Germany. It was one of the ways to withdraw from the hostile environment.

For centuries Jews were a repressed minority, and governing authorities restricted them to low and stagnant positions: they were peddlers, small moneylenders, and cattle dealers. They also had to endure religious persecution, because they were believed to have killed Christ two thousand years ago—the collective guilt they had to carry, a belief that never quite vanished. This religious hatred carried over into daily life, and, long before Hitler came to power, we all had to learn to cope with it.

With no right of appeal, Jews naturally wanted to knock down the fences that restricted them. For generations they had lived in Germany and felt entitled to the same rights the Germans had. In the eighteenth century, when the Enlightenment surged through the western states of Germany, many Jews began to question the status quo. They joined this movement and became liberals and reformists, aiming to change bad conditions and end abuses. (For a majority of Jews, their approach to the world has remained intellectual and reformist liberal. They continued to pass on this liberal attitude to their children even after they had become middle-class. Even today, under different circumstances, it seems to be their prevailing attitude. Although my family's background was "small town," they too subscribed to this liberal view.) However, in the eye of the nationalistic elite that governed Germany, the term *liberal* became a code word by which the Jew was negatively identified, even downgraded, and his claim for liberation rejected.

In Central Europe, the most dramatic change in Jewish life came with the advance of Napoleon's army and the egalitarian principles of the French Revolution. For the first time, full emancipation came to the Jews living in the German territories, but it ended, too soon, with Napoleon's downfall and the rise of a political *Reaktion*.

Throughout the nineteenth century, liberalism and nationalism were the principal trends. During these times of precarious balance, Jews tried to realize some of their expectations. Some village and small town groups moved to larger towns, where they had more possibilities for getting an education and starting businesses. Some of the younger generation had been accepted in German *Gymnasium*s and universities and had entered the professions. Part of them belonged by now to the bourgeois middle class.

But their social role had not changed with the change in their economic status. They were still "separate and half-equal," even though they had lived in Germany for many generations. With the establishment of the German Reich in 1871, antagonistic attitudes toward the Jews did not abate: hostile feelings were held by the new power elite and expressed by all political parties and classes. A new term was coined for this hostility, antisemitism, and from then on was listed in the dictionaries. At the same time, race hatred joined hands with the familiar religious antagonism, and antisemitism thus became a double-edged sword, even more violent than before. When Hitler came to power and adopted antisemitism as the Nazi Party's dogma, he used the word in its double meaning, and it was a deadly mixture.

In 1914, World War I started with the anticipation of victory; nobody could foresee how quickly these hopes would vanish and how deeply this turn of events would affect the lives of the Jews in Germany. In 1914, everybody believed in victory and hoped for a short and glorious war. The kaiser and his government consistently nourished the illusion that Germany was winning the war, when, in fact, everything pointed toward defeat. There were food shortages, and the Germans ate turnips in a time of prolonged deprivation. In 1917, the United States entered the war and added its immense resources to the arsenal of the Allies. The Russians collapsed and were made to sign a bad peace treaty by the German high command. The false impression that Germany was winning the war was created in part because the battles were fought, not on German soil, but on French, Russian, and other enemy territory. The German socialists and liberals demanded that the government conclude a peace without annexations. As late as the middle of 1918, a large final offensive failed, as German reserves could no longer match American resources and manpower, and the German army command was forced into admitting that it had lost the war. The kaiser sued for peace and asked President Wilson to help conclude the war on benevolent terms.

The German people failed to understand why they had lost the war and looked for a scapegoat. The conservative establishment tried to escape their responsibility and engaged in an orgy of antisemitism. Though it had always been present in Germany, in 1918, it was fanned into a political fury of hatred. Thus began a new chapter in German/Jewish relations. Nationalists and returning veterans attacked the Weimar Republic, because it had to fulfill the terms of the victors. Jews, in contrast, supported the Weimar Republic. They saw no sense in continuing a war that was lost and in keeping a regime in power the world considered responsible for the greatest slaughter in human history up to that point. Hitler was part of this national aggression against the Jews, and antisemitism was used to deflect attention from the fact that the nationalists had lost the war. Antisemitism rose and fell in proportion to German prosperity: in the German mind, the Jews remained a potential force for evil.

During these unhappy times, before Hitler came to power, patriotism was elevated to ultranationalism; after he came to power, antisemitism was declared the dogma of the Nazi Party. Every young German—boy or girl—was forced to join the Hitler Youth (*Hitler-Jugend*) and was indoctrinated with hatred for the Jews. The Jews became the "untouchables" of Nazi propaganda, and we all became victims of this propaganda.

Might this destiny of the Jews, which led toward the Holocaust, have changed if the Jews had not been burdened with the image of a pariah for immeasurable times? How much would a change in popular religion have helped to prevent the Holocaust?

A strong defense against these attacks of defamation could not be effected, because Jews were a barely tolerated minority and were too weak. Their only protection against the hostile outer world was to have close family connections. Only the family could be trusted. Written descriptions of the time and documentary films (as, for example, the film *Shoah*) report that Christians could not understand the respect and love a Jewish husband showed toward his wife or her loyalty to him. These close family ties are hard to understand today, because these earlier marriages were often not bonds of love, but marriages of convenience; it was often difficult to find a marriage partner in the small villages in which Jews lived. Frequently, marriages were arranged by a marriage-broker, or by a business friend, as my parents' marriage was. (Only later did I learn how unhappy my mother became when she was forced into marrying my father.)

Marriage also created bonds with the extended family. Many marriages were arranged with men or women who might be helpful in shoring up the family fortune, extending businesses, or, if the need arose, supporting their in-laws. This extended family pattern stretched not only from one place to another in Germany, but also across the European countries and to other continents, as the history of Jewish emigration to the United States proves.

My family was such an extended family, closely knit and mutually supportive. It started in the generation of my maternal grandmother, Jeanette Schöneberg, the youngest child, and her three sisters and two brothers. They lived in a small town in Westphalia, where she was born in 1850. The town was called Salzkotten, so named after the salt works. To judge from the stories I was told or had heard, the Schöneberg sisters were quite a lively tribe. Two of my grandmother's sisters were twins who were so similar in appearance that they had to wear different colored ribbons to be told apart. When they became engaged, they exchanged ribbons and fiancés: it was a most forward game to play for that time. But I guess no serious harm was done, because they were all respectably married in West Germany and Holland. According to my grandmother's own story, she, too, must have been a lively and flirtatious girl. It was with special pride that she told and retold the story of how she was twice selected to be the *Schützenkönigin* (queen of the veterans' shooting contest) of Salzkotten. At that time, in every small German town, a sharp-shooting contest was traditionally held in connection with a general festival called the *Schützenfest*, which took place usually at the end of summer. That was also the time when the *Jahrmarkt* (annual fair) came to town—an assemblage of tents where you could see all kinds of freak shows and strange sights, try your hand at games, watch the "Kasperle" (Punch and Judy show), be whirled around on roller coasters, or see the earth go round from a gondola on the ferris wheel. In short, the Schützenfest was connected with all kinds of merrymaking. I do not mean to take away from my grandmother's honor or her memories of being the *Schützenkönigin* by investing the festival with a vulgar atmosphere. It is well known that the shooting part of the festival was taken seriously in the local community, and, indeed, it must have been an honor for a Jewish girl to have been chosen as *Schützenkönigin*. She was proud of it and attributed her success to her vivaciousness and in greater part to her looks: she was blue-eyed and blonde. Later on, though she loved me dearly, she always wished that I should have looked like her. This particular wish did not vex me—I was familiar with her peculiarities—but I resented it, not for myself, but for my mother, from whom I had inherited my dark eyes and hair. For my mother's sake, I felt bad that grandmother expressed a preference for the German ideal of beauty. I felt that it was offensive toward both my mother and me.

It was good that my grandmother enjoyed her youth, because fate was not too kind to her in later years. She had had many admirers and confessed that she had enjoyed this state of affairs too long and delayed choosing a husband. When she did, she made a "disastrous choice." These were her words. All I ever learned about my grandfather was his family name, Bildesheim. My grandmother did not speak of him, nor did any of the four children. When I asked questions, I was told that they themselves did not know. The last attempt at finding out about this grandfather of mine was in 1967 when Herbert and I were in Courmayeur to visit Uncle Ludwig, the eldest son of this marriage, who was by then eighty-five years old. I should have thought that after so many years he could have taken the skeleton out of the closet but he wouldn't. Therefore, I cannot report anything about my maternal grandfather and can only speculate that he must have been a villain of the worst kind.

Although the four daughters in the Schöneberg family had mostly French names, the two sons had Jewish first names. The older one was Isaac, abbreviated to Is; the younger one was probably Moses, called Max, and in writing abbreviated to M. Uncle M died before I was born. Uncle Is lived to be over ninety years old. My childhood memory of him is that he was tall and somewhat raw-boned, in contrast to his petite wife, Aunt Bertha, whom I liked. They lived in a Westphalian house in the Vielser Strasse in Salzkotten. It was a large house with a half-timbered front, an overhanging roof, and a door that could be opened in four parts to let a horse-drawn carriage drive into the stone-paved interior of the house to unload grain or agricultural produce to be stored in that cavernous space. On the left side of the house were the storage and sales rooms, which, when I explored the house as a child, were empty except for a large scale and weights. To the right were the living quarters. They boasted a surprisingly citified living room, furnished in Biedermeier fashion, the classical-revival style of the first half of the nineteenth century. The room was decorated with little consoles on which urns stood with romantic scenes painted in the Greek style. A lovely grandfather clock hung on the wall. I recall many details of this particular room because I spent many hours in it as a child, usually at the Jewish High Holidays. It was a tradition in our family to visit our grandmother and great-uncle at the time of the holidays. The drive from Wolfenbüttel to Salzkotten by car took only three hours and went through the Teutoburger Wald. Other family members joined us, too, so that we were a large group around the festive table. The Passover Holidays especially left a visual image with me. The "drying room"—at the very back of that old house—contained carved chests in which raiments and pillow cases were stored to be used on the first Seder evening, when Jews celebrate the Exodus of the Children of Israel from Egypt—the old Testament story of how they left as slaves and Moses led them through the Red Sea, when God parted the waters for them. On that evening, a special prayer book, called the "Haggadah," was used, and it had to be read from beginning to end, though it was in Hebrew. We children did not feel excluded because during the meal many old rites took place: bitter herbs were dunked in a special Seder dish and then carefully eaten. At certain moments of the reading, the youngest child, usually my brother, had to ask, "Why is this night different from every other night?" Later on, the children—my brother and I—had to look for the first piece of matzo (unleavened bread) before the blessing could be spoken and the bread broken into many pieces so that everybody could partake in this old ritual. The reading proceeded in the singsong fashion prescribed by tradition, and, though I have not heard them since my childhood, these humming melodies are still in my ears. At this Seder evening, there were at least two readers, to speed up the long prayer, and they were garbed in the old raiments, which were long and white, the front and sleeves ornamented with red and silver piping and beautifully embroidered, and skull caps. We all listened attentively, propped up by special cushions on our chairs. If my memory is reliable, the date embroidered on the pillows was 1754, perhaps proof that the house on the Vielser Strasse in Salzkotten had belonged to the Schöneberg family since that time. On other Jewish High Holidays too, the family gathered in that living room around the table for the meal before we all proceeded together to the synagogue, which was very close by. Though Salzkotten was a small town of no more than five thousand souls, the congregation was alive and closely knit. My mother, especially, enjoyed being in Salzkotten to meet all her old friends, and she showed off her children with much pride.

Uncle, that is, Great-Uncle Is, in whose house we assembled, is the best proof of how integrated the Jews were at the middle of the last century in Westphalia. As a young man, he volunteered to become a soldier in the Prussian army and fought in the War of 1866 against the Bavarians and the Austrians. The Prussians won that war at the famous Battle of Königsgrätz. Again in 1870, he fought with the Prussian army, this time against the French. Again, they were victorious.

On January 18, 1871, the assembled German potentates crowned the king of Prussia as German Emperor William I in the Hall of Mirrors of the Palace of Versailles, near Paris. The German Empire was thus founded on the prostrate body of France, but it fell apart when the same French Republic defeated it in 1918. A peace treaty imposing harsh conditions on the Germans was signed in the same Hall of Mirrors in 1919.

Of course, my great-uncle could not have known all these future events and the bad turns history would take when he enrolled in the Prussian army as a very young man. He was awarded several orders for valor "before the enemy." He was also a member of the Kyffhäuser Bund (a nationalistic war veterans organization) and the founder of the Kriegerverein (a war veterans organization) in Salzkotten. When, in the early 1930s, the Kriegerverein celebrated its sixtieth anniversary, they honored him by driving him through town in an open car, taking him to the parade ground, giving speeches, marching in goosestep, and lowering their flags to him. Through some unknown twists of fate, photos of this event have survived. His medals, too—what an ironic coincidence—were saved, and came into my possession. My great-uncle lived to be ninety years old and died before the Nazis began to deport the Jews to Eastern Europe. Both my grandmother and my great-uncle lived in the Jewish and the German cultures without feeling a break or contradiction.

My grandmother's marriage produced four offspring in short succession: three sons and a daughter, my mother. She was called Johanna, nicknamed Hänschen, the diminutive form of Hans, a German boy's name. The boys' names were Ludwig, Carl, and Ernst. They left Salzkotten early to go to school, and for apprenticeships in commercial careers. Ludwig, the eldest, became a successful businessman in Berlin. Before settling down as a grain merchant in Halle, Carl suffered the fate of so many young German men of his generation: he volunteered at the outbreak of World War I in 1914, and was wounded severely in the battle of the Marne. It took a long time for him to recover. His marriage later added a very elegant woman to our family who came from a Sephardic background. They had one son, Gert, and in 1937 they emigrated to Argentina, where my uncle died two years later. The youngest brother, Ernst, also left Salzkotten early and settled in Berlin. He and a friend tried to build up a textile firm. He married a charming young woman, Hedi, whom I adored. Within the family, we had close ties, and I, as a child and young adult, was always included. There were frequent visits, and my parents' house was the family center: my uncles had married late, and for a long time my brother, Helmut, and I were the only children in the family. I remember my early childhood in Wolfenbüttel as a very happy time.

My grandmother's other brother, Great-Uncle Max, was the first in his generation and our family to step out of the half-rural condition of Salzkotten into an urban environment, changing his life and that of the following generation. He worked for a company in the Rhineland that offered him (and a cousin of his, Carl Paradies) the capital to found and build up a French silk- and lace-importing firm in Berlin. It was called Spitzenhaus M. Schöneberg, after my great-uncle, and for generations it outfitted brides and supplied Berlin dressmakers of that custom-made era with its beautiful silks, at a time when ready-made fashions were unknown. Uncle M died at an early age. I have seen a photo of him: he was an imposing man, elegantly dressed in the mode of the La Belle Époque with a silk top hat, a long black coat, and a black ebony cane with a silver handle, the fashion of the time for gentlemen. I think that he was helpful in assisting my grandmother in her marriage difficulties. I know she adored him and mourned his death until she died thirty-three years later. They are buried side by side in the Jewish cemetery in Berlin-Weissensee.

In my memories, both Salzkotten and my early childhood seem innocent and happy, connected with an image of village life. There was nothing in Salzkotten that you could really call attractive, neither in the little town nor in its environs. Salzkotten had a history going back to the year 1200. The church chronicle reports that the bishop of Paderborn (six miles east of Salzkotten) wanted a fortified town between his diocese and the powerful bishopric of Cologne to protect his borders. He selected the spot because it had the salt works, which had existed since the Middle Ages, and a few *Kotten*, cottages, that had existed since *uralten Zeiten*, time immemorial. So Salzkotten grew into a small town. Then came the Thirty Years' War and with it the Protestant armies that destroyed Salzkotten on St. Thomas's Night in 1633. The church chronicle speaks of "looting and killing—even of children and women. Finally they set it afire." At the end of this chapter, the chronicle closes with the following poem:

> Möge nie der Tag erscheinen,
> Wo die rauhen Kriegeshorden

Dieses stille Tal durchtoben.
Holder Friede, süsse Eintracht
Weilet, weilet freundlich über dieser Stadt.

Roughly translated:

May the day never come,
When the fighting warrior hordes
Are raging through this silent valley,
Blessed peace, sweet harmony
Watch and kindly stay to protect this town.

After the Westphalian Peace Treaty of 1648, the bishop of Paderborn surprisingly retained his diocese and Salzkotten along with it. The town was rebuilt in a helter-skelter way. During my childhood only a few of the old houses on side streets and around the church still stood and they gave Salzkotten the image of an old Westphalian town. The landscape was flat, as if drawn with a ruler. Only one walk led out of town along the *chaussee* (road) that Napoleon built when he marched his conquering armies through Westphalia into Prussia and, finally, into Russia. The *Kilometersteine* (milestones) his armies set still bear witness to the revolutionary zeal of his campaigns across all of Europe. It was a boring walk—I know it from experience—leading to a vegetable garden that belonged to the family, where we spent many afternoons during our summer visits planting all kinds of vegetables. Another, more attractive promenade led us into the *Vielen*, a path between hedgerows leading to a chapel and the landmark Emmaus Linden tree. Often, during Easter time, we went there to pick the violets that grew in profusion along the hedges. Sometimes on these occasions, we saw Catholic processions moving through the hedgerows, the swaying religious statues being carried on the worshipers' shoulders, and we heard their voices intoning in prayer. Another pastime for us children came on washdays. We were equipped with little branches and ordered to stay in the meadow to keep ducks and geese away from the linen sheets bleaching in the sun. As far as I can remember, we never met any of the farm poultry. We watched the wheel of the salt works go around, the current of the little river Heder tugging at the low-hanging branches of the willows, and smelled the scent of fresh green meadows. We also had the great northern sky, a landscape such as Rembrandt has drawn with a few lines giving the impression of vastness. Who can say when my interest and admiration for landscape painting really started? There are probably many such question marks; at least I, at the time of the bleachery green in Salzkotten, was not aware of such future impressions. I was much more attracted to places where some action took place: *die Freiheit*, a little square where the smithy shod the horses, with the anvil bellows, the hammering sound on metal, and the comings-and-goings of people and carriages; or baker Hölter's door, where I could see the loaves of bread coming out of the oven, baked to a crusty brown, smelling deliciously, making me hungry for a buttered slice of it. But the highlight of summer visits in Salzkotten was always an outing to the medieval castle, Wewelsburg, in horse-drawn carts (*Leiterwagen*) to have a picnic and play games in the meadow under the then famous Parapluie trees, umbrella pines. Old and young came, family and friends, and we returned home happy and exhausted.

Only many years later, I learned from a memorial volume published by a Bonn government agency that my childhood playground had become notorious in the fantasy land of the Third Reich. Hitler and Himmler had turned it into an educational center for their future elites: SS Führer Himmler's SS leaders were indoctrinated in the new German religion of race theories. They abandoned Christianity and followed pagan German rites instead. Himmler had chosen the Wewelsburg to enact his absurd Teutonic mythology and had created a nearly operatic cult, a circle of "SS Knights," resembling "King Arthur's Court," a mere figment of Teutonic fantasies that helped them perpetrate the Holocaust in words, then in deeds. The new mythology elevated one type of human being, and made pariahs of all others. Yes, this new totem pole had gradations of inferiority; without a doubt, the Jews occupied the lowest rank. They were rated lower than dogs. Dogs, though animals, could become man's best friend and were, therefore, valuable. Jews, in contrast, had to be feared for many reasons. The theory was based on two contradictory lies about Jews: on one hand, the Nazis considered them of racially inferior blood; on the other, they believed that Jews were extremely powerful and aimed at controlling the world. Democracy they considered a Jewish trick, an ideology that would allow these inferior Jews, with their exceptional cunning, to lord it over others. Especially by Hitler and Himmler, the Jewish threat was perceived as against the German race, because the Jews could spoil Aryan purity by marrying into it. Therefore, the racial laws of 1935 forbade such marriages. Not only did intermarriage become a crime, but also interracial relationships, which were punishable, and ended for the Jewish partner in a concentration camp. Only women older than forty-five—past childbearing age—could be employed in Jewish households. But soon even that could not take place. The incessant Nazi propaganda against Jews in Germany was so pervasive that no official contact between Jews and other Germans was possible any longer and could exist only in secret. The goal of every German state, town, and village was to be free of the Jews, *judenrein*. Beside the name signs of towns or villages was a second sign proclaiming that the town was *judenrein*! But that was not enough for Hitler and Himmler; those Teutonic race maniacs pursued their "Aryan race theory" to the conclusion that Jews were vermin and therefore should be exterminated. SS Führer Himmler consigned this task to his elite SS troops. They could be commanded to handle this onerous task: or, rather, they were the only ones to be entrusted to kill the Jews—all the Jews—in a systematic way, because for them such killing was not abhorrent, as it might have been to others. They felt that their moral superiority could not be disturbed by simple human mercy. In fact, to preclude such pity, Himmler was known to have given pep talks to the SS before and after mass killings of Jews.

But not only had the Wewelsburg served to disseminate the Teutonic myth: from May 1939 until 1943, it also housed a concentration camp. Himmler had imagined the Wewelsburg as "the center of the Germanic world," and for this purpose he started to rebuild the castle with slave laborers. It did not work out his way. Himmler's mad illusions had to be given up when—after the first massive defeats of the German armies—armament projects were given priority.

"Until that time—1943—3,900 prisoners had passed through this small and independent concentration camp. . . . [M]any of the prisoners died of hard labor in the stone quarries, and nearly one-third (1,285) were executed: the largest group were Soviet Russians and Poles; many of the German prisoners belonged to the international religious Organization of Jehovah's Witnesses. . . . [I]n 1945, mass executions took place in a small forest near the Wewelsburg." It was a gruesome sequel to my childhood memories.

My early childhood memories of Salzkotten were very happy ones: I felt contained within the family circle, and it was important that I had playmates my own age. While I was in Salzkotten, I was included in the throng of young children, sharing most of their activities, even accompanying them to their school sometimes. This was the Jewish elementary school—the same one my mother had graduated from—located in the synagogue. Going to school was fun for me, because they had, at this time, a young and attractive teacher, and the class was lively. The building was located on a small square, surrounded by other old and narrow buildings. I remember, too, that it had a rickety staircase, which I climbed up usually on Yom Kippur to bring flowers to Omi and Aunt Bertha at the time the prayers for the Seelenfeier (prayers for the dead) were read.

My mother, too, was happy to renew the ties of her youth in Salzkotten. It was an animated time with all the visits to be made and then reciprocated. The evenings held their own memories, because my grandmother was an inventive storyteller, and so my brother and I besieged her for more. The scene is still before my eyes: in her living room, right before the window, was an elevated platform. There stood her comfortable grandmother's chair, her sewing table, and two little footstools for us. We sat at her feet waiting for the best-loved story, which she had to repeat and repeat—the story of a lost soldier returning home from the war. Usually this long hour ended at dusk and the day, too, had its happy ending.

A few years later the scene changed; my playmates had left Salzkotten to continue their schooling in different places. My grandmother, too, had left; although she still kept her apartment, she lived most of the time with us in Wolfenbüttel. Salzkotten had lost its attraction.

During the summer of 1968, when Herbert and I were in Europe, we witnessed how deeply any memory of the Jews in Salzkotten had been repressed. At Uncle Ludwig's suggestion, we visited Salzkotten to see if the graves of the Schöneberg family were well cared for. Uncle Ludwig could not visit the graves himself, as he had always done—he was eighty-six years old and did not travel easily any longer. He told us where to get the key to the cemetery. We soon found out that no key was necessary, because the fence of the cemetery had been demolished and many of the gravestones stood on the narrow cobblestone street. On one part of the cemetery grounds, a new factory had been built, and the gravestones removed; the other part of the cemetery was neglected. Our visit took place on a gray and drizzly afternoon, and it felt as if the weather deepened our gloom. On we went to the place where the synagogue once stood; we found an empty space. Everything had been thoroughly cleaned up, not a stone of the foundation to be seen. The little square had been macadamized. Where the synagogue once stood, there was a *Litfassäule*, a German-type round billboard with advertisements for businesses and movie schedules. Unlike in other German villages and towns, no memorial tablet recalled that there was once a Jewish house of worship in this place. Anger about this indignity left me deeply frustrated: first they killed the Jews and then they killed their memory.

We could not leave the situation as we had found it; something had to be done. Our first step took us to the Catholic parish priest. He lived in the village beside the central church. His was a typical house, with a well-cared-for garden. The word *neat* came to my mind. This care for material things pacing my memories of murder were all I could think of. The priest was a punctilious man of middle age and as polite and noncommittal in manner as possible—a man, so he told us, who was new and without power in his congregation. This visit made us sadder than we had been before. We found out that the mayor of the town was a florist, and we went to see him. His wife refused us access. It was like coming to a stone wall, cold and silent: humanity denied again! A last possibility was to speak to the owner of the bread factory, Mr. Reinecke, the richest and most influential man in Salzkotten. Well, yes, he would receive us. Yes, he did remember my family, and though he could not promise he could do anything, having retired long ago from all the official positions he had held in the town administration, he would try to do something. Herbert and I both had the impression that he was a considerate man who could be reached by our appeal. Our visit in Salzkotten almost at an end, I knew that I would never return. I still wanted to do one thing, though: walk once more through the Vielser Strasse, where the house of my great-uncle still stood. But it did not revive memories I could feel at peace with, not now, not ever. The events at the cemetery disturbed me greatly and destroyed my happy memories of the past.

At the hour of leave-taking I knew that only one thing remained to be done—to find the path to the hedgerow, the Vielen, and I wanted to do it alone. It was easy to find, and for a few minutes I walked along the hedges, where my mother must have walked when she was a young girl and happy, and where she took us to pick violets. At this time there were no violets to pick, so I picked a small twig of spirea and left.

Two years after our visit, I was told in New York by a friend, the lawyer Arnold Oswald, who was from Salzkotten, that the Jewish cemetery there had been restored. Too late for Uncle Ludwig: he died a year after our visit.

In 1986, the billboard in the empty square once filled by the synagogue was removed. The outline of the destroyed synagogue, built in 1825, is now marked by two walls. A memorial plaque, with the Star of David, quotes the Bible: "Put off thy shoes, for the place whereon thou standest is holy ground" (Exodus 3:5). Could our visit have enlightened the city fathers about their duty to the dead?

One Jewish family from Salzkotten, the Goldschmidts, survived in Argentina, and one member of the Oswald family lived in New York.

To recall the town chronicle, it never so much as mentions that Jews had had ever lived there:

Blessed peace, sweet harmony,
Watch and kindly stay to protect this town!

2

Going to School: Wolfenbüttel, 1920–1933

MY FATHER'S FAMILY, the Schlosses, lived in Wolfenbüttel. We considered ourselves homegrown. The town was our home; we knew no other. Yet our roots were rather short, as we learned with time. Our grandfather had been born and raised in another state, the Grand Duchy of Hesse, and had migrated north only at the end of the nineteenth century. Wolfenbüttel is a small town. Little is known about its general history and, though it reaches back into the Middle Ages, even less about the history of the Jews in Wolfenbüttel.

On an old map we own by Johann Baptist Homan of the eighteenth century of the Ducatus Brunsuicensis—the Duchy of Braunschweig—my hometown is shown as a large red dot surrounded by fortress-like outcroppings. The town sits astride a river flowing north, the Oker. The surrounding area is colored in light beige, an indication of a slight elevation; to the north one can observe a marked green line, running horizontally: the beginning of the North German Plain, all in green and extending all the way to the North and Baltic Seas.

Wolfenbüttel was a garrison town, though the stone and earthen walls have long been razed and made into public parks, creating a green belt around the inner town, inviting a *Spaziergang*, a walk. To the little river, the Oker, the town owes some of its romantic feeling; a side arm surrounds the castle like a moat and creates little canals in town. One canal, called the *Stadtgraben*, was covered with water lilies during the summer and provided skating grounds for the youth of Wolfenbüttel in the winter. The many wooded areas, ridges of the Harz Mountains, furnished some of the building material for Wolfenbüttel's half-timbered houses, a German building style since the Middle Ages.

These beautiful forests of beeches were within walking distance of town. On Sunday afternoons, parents gathered up children and grandparents, all in their Sunday finery, for an outing. Soon, a procession of old and young would make their way up the Neue Weg toward the Lechlumer Wald. The children were bribed to pick wood anemones, or little boys would shake *Maikäfer* from the trees, so that they could scare little girls with them, or they would play a game of tag called *Wechsele das Bäumchen*. When everybody was out of breath, they would repair to a nearby garden restaurant to recuperate with ice cream and cake.

The town's closeness to the North German Plain was, of course, its single important feature, because it gave the town its livelihood. For centuries, its fertile soil had been tilled, planted, and harvested: it yielded a great variety of agricultural products that determined its commercial stability.

In my youth I was not concerned with Wolfenbüttel's viability, but from early on, I recognized the surroundings of Wolfenbüttel as being beautiful. From the slight elevation of the Lechlumer Wald, one had a wide view over the plain, and, according to the season, one could see the workers busy in the fields, almost like a Van Gogh painting. At other times a mist hung over the ground; then the whole wide plain disappeared, as if it had never been there.

Wolfenbüttel was a sleepy jewel of a town in its ancient architecture. Its foundation and development were intimately linked with its rulers: the dukes of Braunschweig and Wolfenbüttel. They had built their fortification and the castle, as well as a moat and the half-timbered town houses, that give Wolfenbüttel its charm and character. Unlike other places in Germany, the history of the ducal house did not extend into the Middle Ages, though its name Wolfenbüttel, in ancient history, is connected with the House of the Guelphs, *das Haus der Welfen*. The dukes of Braunschweig moved to Wolfenbüttel, then an insignificant fortification, and for about three hundred years, until 1753, they made Wolfenbüttel their residence. Its Renaissance and Baroque princes built new churches, refurbished the castle in Baroque style, and set up their courtiers and staff in charming rows of small houses that lined streets and squares.

The town's enduring claim to fame was not its court culture, though the dukes set up a theater and attracted famous musicians to their court. In the middle of the seventeenth century, a large library was built by a Renaissance-style prince, Duke August, as a monument to scholarship and to the universal mind of a prince who rebuilt the town after the Thirty Years' War. Duke August's successors kept building up the town, but apparently they were the only dynamic element to make Wolfenbüttel into a flourishing town. It was overtaken by Braunschweig, whose citizens successfully strove for progress in culture and commerce.

In the middle of the eighteenth century, the dukes moved the entire court and its administration to Braunschweig. From that moment on, everything stood still in Wolfenbüttel. The Duke August Library sank into a deep sleep and lost all intellectual ambitions. The town became so poor that half its inhabitants left, and the rest endured impoverishment for almost a century. When the ducal house departed from Wolfenbüttel so precipitously, it not only left the townspeople to deal with extreme economic hardship, but also dealt a blow to their pride which was hard for them to forget. Fifty years later, when Napoleon conquered Germany and set up the Kingdom of Westphalia, which included the duchy, it was felt as a further lowering of national and provincial self-esteem. Not until the end of the nineteenth century—at the time when my grandfather settled his family in Wolfenbüttel—did the town develop ways to overcome economic stagnation and recover a sufficient sense of balance to build up the administrative, cultural, and educational aspect of the town and participate in the general growth the peaceful times before World War I afforded.

However, this positive development came to an abrupt end when, in 1918, World War I was lost, the ducal house, like all princely and royal houses in Germany, was deposed, and Germany became a republic, the Weimar Republic.

I referred earlier to the national consequences of these catastrophic events. On a local level, my family's immediate concern, the consequences were no less threatening. The glory of the past stood in stark relief to the impoverished conditions the people had to endure. The contrast between past and present turned them into German nationalists who rejected liberal government and culture as well as the Weimar Republic. Earlier than all other German states they voted for the Nazi Party and supported Hitler as the Führer of the German Reich. (Even as a schoolgirl, I realized that the ideas of the Weimar Republic had not been accepted by many of my teachers.)

During the seventeenth and eighteenth centuries Wolfenbüttel had a very different spirit. In order to plan the library, Duke August had attracted one of the greatest German thinkers to come there. Gottfried Wilhelm von Leibniz was the duke's principal adviser in assembling a library; he also served as a consultant to its architect, and the success of the building, a graceful rotunda, was credited to him. During the second part of the eighteenth century, Gotthold Ephraim Lessing became the librarian. He was the poet of the Enlightenment and wrote his famous play *Nathan der Weise* while he was living in Wolfenbüttel. It contains the universally known three-ring parable: which of the religions is true, Christianity, Judaism, or Islam? The play is set in Jerusalem during the Crusades, a period of fanaticism when the Jewish religion was held in abhorrence, wars were fought in the name of "the one true religion," and all others were condemned to destruction.

The story goes like this: a wise sultan named Saladin poses this question to the equally wise Nathan: which of the world's religions does he consider the true and authentic one? Nathan resolves the dilemma by responding with a parable: a father, having only one ring, loves his three sons equally well and decides before his death to have two rings made in a likeness so perfect that one could not tell the difference. Upon the father's death, each son receives a ring, but nobody can claim to possess the original one. Saladin understands the moral of the eighteenth-century Enlightenment: religions are different forms of a core truth regarding man's relationship to God. In this way, Lessing makes Nathan the Jew into a representative of the Enlightenment, where tolerance is the accepted principle of judgment. Modern Jewish thinking, however, has recognized that Lessing's Enlightenment thesis was flawed, because it puts restrictions on the Jew, who can be completely free only if he strives to give up his separateness. Lessing's ideal Jew was only marginally Jewish.

In 1929, the town invented a "Lessing Year," during which the cycle of Lessing's plays were performed in a theater named after him. To enhance Wolfenbüttel's reputation, they fused his illustrious name with that of the town. It became "Wolfenbüttel, die Lessingstadt"! The invoking of his name a few short years before "Hitler's brown masses" came to power and murdered with fanatical intolerance has made me see Wolfenbüttel and its people as thorough hypocrites. It also should be said that Lessing felt unhappy and lonely in Wolfenbüttel during the last years of his life: he dubbed Wolfenbüttel a cultural backwater—*Krähwinkel*—and spent much of his time with friends in Braunschweig. He died there, and nobody knows where he is buried: Lessing, symbol of the Enlightenment, a forgotten man.

My grandfather, Liebmann Schloss, told me late in his life that his family had lived in a small village of Zimmersrode in the State of Hesse during most of the nineteenth century. This region had many Jewish settlements, most of them poor. His family, the Schlosses, were numerous, and at the end of the century he and his younger brother Nathan, made the decision to leave Zimmersrode with their families to look for better economic and cultural conditions someplace else. His choice fell on Wolfenbüttel. He did not tell me why he preferred it to other places. In doing so, he followed a general trend of this period, when many Jewish families pulled up their roots in the countryside and moved to larger villages and towns. My grandfather came from a Jewish village milieu. Jewish life was based on Jewish piety and was tightly knit; the decision to leave familiar surroundings must have been a daring step to take. When grandfather and his brother made the choice to move, they were grown men and had to weigh carefully the conditions they and their families would encounter in a new environment. There was no doubt that he wanted to continue to live in a Jewish world, and have close contact with other Jews—who else would have accepted them anyway?—and a Jewish education for his three young sons.

What my grandfather knew of Jewish life in Wolfenbüttel I cannot say. I have no letter or other personal documents to consult. The congregation he joined there was a small one. Before the nineteenth century, only some rich court Jews and their large households had been admitted for residence. Approximately one hundred years before my family came, no more than forty or fifty Jews were settled there, most of them of middling wealth or poor. A local historian speaks of the great contrast between the court Jews and the underprivileged, which included many extremely poor itinerants or peddlers. Most of the attention Wolfenbüttel received at that time the Jews owed to a Talmud-Thora school, founded in 1786 by the family of a court Jew named Philipp Samson.

When my grandfather came to Wolfenbüttel, he enrolled his three sons in that school, which by then had become a *Real Schule* (a high school with emphasis on languages and science) and had graduated some famous Jewish scholars. They included Leopold Zunz, who became an outstanding founder of Wissenschaft des Judentums (a scholarly and liberal reform movement among Jews), and such famous educators as Samuel M. Ehrenberg and Israel Jacobson. This reputation seems to indicate that my grandfather wanted not only to escape the straitened circumstances of the village he came from, but also to give his children the best German and Jewish education available in this part of the country. He sent his sons to the Samsonschule, which at that time had acquired a reputation all over Germany; my brother, Helmut, born in 1915, was also enrolled in that school. As a girl, I was not admitted, but my father took me to commemorative services and to social events. I remember well when my father took me to a "ball" at the school, where I danced my first waltz with him.

Strangely enough, there must have been a lack of coordination between the Samsonschule and the Wolfenbüttel *Gemeinde* (congregation). Three years before the Samsonschule moved to larger quarters, the congregation had built a large synagogue next to our house. But the seats of the synagogue were never filled, because the Samsonschule had its own private prayer rooms in its new building.

At the end of the 1920s the school was forced to close when it lost money invested in war bonds, which had become valueless, and inflation destroyed its capital. After 1945, the Samsonschule building was taken over by the town and used as a police academy. Recently, it was converted to a craft and trade school for apprentices.

The relative prosperity of our family was based on our grandfather and his brother, who founded a long-distance trade in
draft oxen and horses. They bought the animals in markets situ-
ated in East Frisia and Saxony and shipped them by railroad to
Wolfenbüttel. Their business was located close to the railroad
station. My father and his brother inherited the business, which,
they felt, served the needs of the peasants of that area. In my
generation, the Schlosses were an extended family in Wolfenbüttel: I had ten first and second cousins in town. We often played
in the large courtyard and hayloft in the Brothers Schloss's business complex in the Halchterstrasse. Most of us in the second
generation succeeded in saving ourselves from Nazi Germany
and emigrated in time. One of my second cousins, Joachim
Domp, whose family had transferred its piano factory to Holland, was tragically caught and killed while he served in the
Dutch resistance against Nazi occupation. After the war, the
family exchanged letters between Switzerland, Holland, England, Australia, Chile, and Argentina.

The household was set up for the kind of life that placed a big
burden on the woman of the house, my mother, as was the custom at that time. My mother had taken on this task with special
eagerness which, I think was a constant in her life: caring for her
family, as she was used to doing from an early age. I believe that
it compensated her for the many hardships in her life.

Before they had moved into the house in the Lessingstrasse,
she had made sure that she would have a comfortable and "hy-
gienic" kitchen. Because baking was her hobby, she had a good-
size baking oven installed. (In the 1930s, she and I learned from
a real pâtissier how to make fancy pastry and chocolate truffles
in preparation for an emigration that never materialized.) The
kitchen also had a special Grude oven, heated with finely
ground coals, which made it possible to maintain a slow-burn-
ing fire at a low temperature. It was my mother's constant ambi-
tion to give my father a warm meal when he returned late from
an overland trip and to serve a well-prepared hot dinner at our
family reunions. I retain a warm picture of her, as a busy and
caring provider, canning fruit and vegetables, pickling meat,
and putting eggs in a glassy mixture to be used during the winter months. Fall was one of her busiest periods, when baskets of

fruit had to be stored in the cellar or *Pflaumenmus* (prune butter) had to be cooked in a large copper kettle. At regular intervals a washerwoman would come and for three days organize our household around the laundry room.

Since we lived close to the synagogue, my parents received weekly visits after the Sabbath service or during the High Holidays, and my mother enjoyed her well-deserved reputation as an hospitable hostess and for the stimulating conversation around her table. She was fond of literature and had developed, among others, a special taste for the North-German humorist Fritz Reuther, who wrote in his native Platt-deutsch. I still recall that she often was amused by him. She also enjoyed the theater and rarely missed a performance in the newly built Lessing Theater. At least once a year, she accepted an invitation from her oldest brother, who was still a bachelor, to take in "gay Berlin." But amid all these activities and diverse interests, she was also an avid newspaper reader and became aware, earlier than others, of signs of danger in postwar German politics.

My mother's brothers and their families frequently visited us from Halle and Berlin. It was at these family festivities that my mother produced true culinary feasts. Fortunately, she had some help preparing for these festive occasions from the sleep-in maids we had through all these years. They came from the surrounding villages and stayed on for years. They became very close and were treated almost like family members. At *Weihnachten*, they got their own little Christmas trees and gifts from each member of the family.

At that time, it was an accepted custom in rural families to have their daughters become accomplished in the ways a town household was managed and earn some money toward their marriage dowries. I think that my mother was generous with them and also a good and patient teacher. I do not remember the hiring process exactly, but I do know that we had no trouble finding village families who were glad to have their daughters serve in our household. Apparently, relationships at that level were not tinged by antisemitism—or, at least not yet.

Anna, the first maid I remember, came from Thiede, a neighboring village. She helped in bringing us up, and we were saddened when she left our household to marry. Her sister Minna took her place and adopted our family as hers. She, too, left to marry after having spent many years with us. One of my vivid childhood recollections falls into this Anna–Minna period. Their older brother came in regular intervals to visit them. He appeared as an overwhelming presence in our kitchen, not only because he was a large man but because he wore the blue uniform of the gendarme of Thiede and a *Pickelhaube* (a spiked helmet) which was awe-inspiring to a small child. Remembering the scene in our kitchen now, more than seventy years later, I am struck by its resemblance to the stage setting of an opera buffa, entirely comical. Nevertheless, he was a friendly man, and his smile could diminish the fear of one small girl to the vanishing point.

My brother and I were happy and secure in the embrace of this caring family. Helmut was younger than I by two years and would frequently toddle after me when I attended kindergarten and visited friends. He would even climb aboard a streetcar to reach me when my first-grade class went on an outing. When we were toddlers, we played around the house and garden; a swing dangled from one of the apple trees and there was a *Laube* (arbor) for the quieter summer hours. We dreaded the daily nap time and tried hard to avoid it unless we were coaxed into it by promises of a story. I did not like Hoffman's Struwwelpeter (Raggedy Peter), a little boy who did not want to eat and was punished. I hated the idea of punishment because I, too, was a picky eater. Nor did I like Wilhelm Busch's most famous story, centered in two characters named Max and Moritz. Only some of the fairy tales by the brothers Grimm or Hans Christian Andersen did the job.

Later on, our favorites changed. One of the family's guests had brought a book along as a gift for me: it had even a little poem as a dedication to me. It was a collection of animal stories, and we loved them. From that point on, it was Sven Hedin's adventure stories that held our attention. When we grew older, my brother's and my own interests differed: I got into "*Jung-Mädchen Literatur*," such as "Nesthäkchen," and my brother preferred adventure stories such as those by Karl May. Both of us loved James Fenimore Cooper's *The Last of the Mohicans*, which fascinated everybody. Other aspects of Americana I added in my early teens by reading *Tom Sawyer*: Aunt Polly's character and the whitewashing of the fence created amusing imagery in my mind, like a tableau vivante to smile at. Some of these images contrasted in mood with those of *Uncle Tom's Cabin*.

It was not until I came to the United States and brought you up, Janie, that I came to appreciate English and American children's literature. As a young mother, I received an education on how to bring up a child on the "new continent." Everything was new to me. As I read Mother Goose to you, Janie, their funny rhymes and playfulness were a wonderful entertainment for both of us. Many of the stories I read to you stressed the humorous and positive side of things, in strong contrast to the children's literature in Germany, which aimed at being didactic and threatening. I especially liked *The Little Engine That Could*. This little engine could overcome all obstacles on its way as it puffed up the mountainside. I must have read it a hundred times: it always felt like a great triumph when the little engine arrived at the mountain peak.

It seemed to me that children in the United States were viewed and treated entirely differently from what had been the custom in Germany. One book in the 1920s was even entitled *The Century of the Child*. Children were seen as little treasures, whatever the burden of bringing them up. Their development was watched over carefully and, to my surprise, every mother used the same book to guide the stages of this development. I had never seen this approach in Europe: children were brought up as mother had done before, and there was no doubt that our culture and our customs gave us a model we did not question for quite some time. When the other mothers and I sat in the playground on Central Park West and 100th Street, and compared notes, we were satisfied that Dr. Spock's prescription for bringing up children was the most "modern and scientific" way to do it right: a bible for young mothers. I am not sure, though, that we always followed Dr. Spock's advice on setting up timetables for a young child. Herbert saw his youth as dominated by traditional authority and wanted to bring you up as free as possible in a free country. I leave it to you, Janie, to decide if we succeeded.

In Wolfenbüttel, as my brother and I became pre-schoolers,

we discovered that we did not have any playmates in our neighborhood. A veterinarian's family occupied the lower floor of the
house, and it included a daughter my age, but there was no
contact between our families, and whenever we appeared down-
stairs to play the daughter was called in by her mother. I learned
later that my parents saw this as a clear sign of antisemitism. But
my parents had good relations with the party living on the
upper floor, Mrs. Baars, a war-widow.

As soon as I could be trusted to cross the street and watch out
for my brother, we frequently went to Halchterstrasse to play
with our four cousins and later in the afternoon to pick up our
father to walk home with him. (That he might stop on the way
at the Sarotti chocolate store was a point of interest to us that we
did not let him forget.) We spent the hours in the Halchterstrasse
mostly in playing with a throng of children in an open space
without parental supervision. It was equal fun, however, to be
part of the large family headed by Uncle Nathan and his wife,
Aunt Lene. I came to like my uncle for his even temper and
developed a special relationship with my aunt. She took me seriously beyond my years and later, when I was a teenager, chan-
neled my natural curiosity to the larger world of literature and
politics. I kept up a lively relationship with two of my cousins
after they emigrated to England.

When my brother got older, he dropped out of our little play
group: we were all girls, and, like his father, whose easygoing
temperament he had inherited, he turned his interest to automo-
biles. My father took several trips to Rüsselsheim to buy a late-
model Opel from the factory and drove it all the way to Wolfenbüttel by himself. He was the only driver in the family, although
we did have an "historic" chauffeur named Gustav Kalweit, who
had driven General Hindenburg while he was commanding
German armies in World War I.

This early "automania" would influence my brother all his
life. He was taught how to drive cars by my father and big trucks
by Gustav. When he emigrated to Israel, he was detached to
drive heavy agricultural machinery in his kibbutz, Givat Brenner. In 1937, he drove armored personnel vehicles for the British
military police, and when he shifted to the Jewish defense forces,
he was sent on fairly dangerous missions into Arab territory.

The rest of his life he spent as a greatly respected member of the Bus Cooperative Egged, passing his passion for cars on to his own children. During the several wars that have plagued Israel since the foundation of the state, he was drafted into the army reserve and transported troops and supplies to different fronts. We saw each other frequently in Israel, and he and his wife, Susi, came to visit us in New York. In some years, we coordinated our vacations in Europe with theirs so that we could spend some time together and visit the Jewish cemetery in Wolfenbüttel. He would still regularly buy his Opels in the Federal Republic of Germany and take them along to Israel, where he lived with his family in his well-tended house and garden in Kiryat Bialik near Haifa. He had transformed a one-room accommodation on a sandy lot into a respectable one-family dwelling. He died in 1991 and was laid to rest in Israeli earth after a full life, far from the persecutions in which his parents were murdered and the community of his youth destroyed.

School

I entered school when I was seven years old. Because I was born in August, I missed the cut-off date for six-year-olds. I had been waiting with anticipation and some apprehension for school to start, because my parents tried to prepare me by telling me that going to school would demand more responsibility and admonishing me to do well in school because it might be important for my future. The concept of "future" was somehow nebulous for a seven-year-old, but I was eager to learn and curious about what school would be like. And it was good that in preparing me for school this way my parents did not anticipate that I, or any child, could be frightened about going. The educational theory of the time was that children had to accept naturally the realities of life, because they were thought of as little adults doing what was reasonable.

When the day came, it was a sad day for me and my family. My mother was taken ill: she had to have an operation and was in serious condition in the hospital. When we children were admitted for a short time to the sickroom, we were allowed only to whisper a few endearing words to her. The whole family waited anxiously for her recovery. When the doctor declared her out of danger, we felt happy to have our mommy back and could return to our natural voices and behavior. It was a reassuring feeling that she was home again.

Because of her sickness, she could not take me to school on my first day, so a neighbor accompanied me. I felt very lonely carrying my *Schultüte* and my book satchel, the equivalent of a small rucksack. Getting a *Schultüte* on your first day of school is still a German custom. It is unknown in the United States. I looked up the word in the dictionary and found a rather long explanation of it as "a conical bag of sweets given to children on their first day of school."

Although very close to my home, my school was not a regular school, at least not in the usual sense: it was in a wing of the castle that the dukes of Braunschweig and Wolfenbüttel had left in 1753. Its official name was Anna Vorwerk Oberlyzeum, but in daily language it was called *die Schloßschule*, the castle school.

In 1977, the origins of the school were described by the vice mayor, Heinz Grunow in a brochure entitled "Wolfenbüttel: History in Pictures." "After the princely house had left Wolfenbüttel, the Castle decayed and nobody cared for its upkeep. The Palace came very near to be[ing] sold at demolition value during the time of King Jérome Kassel (he was Napoleon's brother and king of Westphalia). But a last-minute intervention was successful and the palace was made a gift to the town of Wolfenbüttel by Royal Decree of June 5, 1813. . . . To preserve such a monumental building over a long period of time, a sound economic basis for its use had to be provided. Certainly, it was not easy to find such a basis for the Palace, which had served nothing but representational purposes of a ruling dynasty for centuries.

"Anna Vorwerk, a lady teacher who was looking for a space to be used as a nursery school and other pedagogical institutions, vividly described what she found in the middle of the 19th century: 'The massive building lay huddled and seemingly inaccessible, dark and decayed, the statues on the bridges decapitated. . . . the interior, if you believed the vivid imagination of young people, was inhabited by roaming ghosts . . . putting in an appearance at midnight . . .—but, at least, there were all kinds of big rooms to be had for the asking.' "

The vice mayor continues: "Anna Vorwerk was not to be deterred by the desolate state of the old place. Her requirements were extremely modest, and the rooms were made available free of charge; she had them renovated at her own expense and started a nursery school, three elementary grades, and a teacher's seminary. These were the modest beginnings of what came to be a well-known school for girls that celebrated its 100th anniversary in 1966. Today it is known as the 'Gymnasium im Schloß,' the largest of Wolfenbüttel's three high schools all on a co-educational basis."

When I entered the school, it was a *Lyzeum* or *Gymnasium* and had nine grades leading to the *Abitur* (matriculation examination). I had to go through three years of private elementary school though, but such schools were dissolved when the *Volksschule*, the public elementary school, was introduced. Attached to the school was a ladies' teacher seminary where young women from "good" families—the German status word is *Höhere Töchter*—were educated to become teachers of other aspiring young women during a time when the women's movement was still in its infancy and not many professions were open to them.

The curriculum was that of a *Real-Gymnasium* with the stress on foreign languages. In the lower grades we received instructions in German, especially German grammar, and as the beginning of German history, we started off with the German epic of the *Nibelungen Lied,* a conscious effort to strengthen our German national identity, when we were ten or eleven years old: German hero-worship during the Weimar Republic! Two years later French and English lessons were added on a daily schedule. We were also taught Greek and Roman history and read the *Iliad* and the *Odyssey* in class; this gave me a basic grounding in ancient history. In the upper grades, regular courses in higher mathematics (algebra) and physics were added: I remember a lesson in the physics room—a specially equipped room for experiments—when our teacher, Herr Dr. Kössler, explained the chain reaction that takes place in an atomic explosion and filled our minds with the horrors of a world conflagration.

To round off our education, we also had music and drawing

lessons: it was fun to sit in the Schloß-Garten sketching a window overgrown with vines and the sun filtering through the trees. But these drawing lessons, nice as they were, did not have any connection with art: they were mere exercises in skill. Art history was not in the curriculum at a time when the French Impressionists had created new and different ways of seeing reality and in Germany the Blaue Reiter Gruppe was revolutionizing the art world. We in the Schloßschule knew nothing of this development, which happened in our time. Why this omission? Were art and art history not recognized as serious subjects, or was it a rejection of a modern development that ten years later made the style of the *Blaue Reiter* into *Entartete Kunst*?

Our French reader, Börner-Mitell, contained in each of its many volumes (first to seventh grade) a color reproduction by the Swiss painter Puvis de Chavannes. He favored the idealization of antiquity, a somewhat anemic style of classicism. I recognize his paintings immediately when they are shown in a museum and am reminded of the "French lesson."

I should also mention that we had gymnastics and that the school participated in the annual *Turnfest* (gymnastic display). The town's school population paraded through town—everybody had to wear white tops and black shorts—and then assembled on the *Sportfeld* for a demonstration of the gymnastics we had been drilled in. The speeches honored *Turnvater Jahn* (Friedrich Ludwig Jahn, called the founder of German national gymnastics), and the accompanying brass band played Johannes Brahm's symphonic version of *Gaudeamus igitur*. It was an occasion to make every national heart beat with pride.

The nationalistic upper crust of families in the city dominated our town—they were the powers that be. The Revolution of 1918 had left the old military garrison in place. One of its commanding officers was the later infamous Commander General Keitel, sentenced to death for war crimes at the Nuremberg trials in 1946. His daughter Erika was one of my classmates. In addition, the city had become the seat of the district-government, the *Regierungsbezirk*. The military officers, the higher officials, and a few landowning families dominated the social and political climate. They also gave the educational institutions like the *Schloßschule* their cultural cachet.

Ultranationalists, like the director, Dr. Gertrud Hasse, and her leading staff members, followed a conservative agenda: from the Middle Ages on to World War I, they taught us about German victories in battle and successes overseas. The disintegration of the German Reich, following the defeat and loss of their colonies in Africa in 1918, was not mentioned in our history lessons; the establishment of the Weimar Republic was suppressed; and our teachers flaunted their opposition to the Republic. I gained the impression, in contrast to the views at home, that the new republic was repugnant to many of my teachers. They yearned for *tempi passati*.

A good example of ultraconservative thinking among our teachers was our French teacher, the elderly Fräulein Schmidt. She was an ethnic German from the Baltic states (*Volksdeutsche vom Baltikun*) and wore her *deutsch-nationale* (ultranationalist) opposition on her sleeve. Sometimes, our lessons were used for political discussion: indoctrination pure and simple! Once, I was ordered to read aloud before the class an editorial of a well-known conservative newspaper for having been so "unpatriotic" as to express a "yes vote" for "bread" in the then raging *Volksentscheid* (referendum) discussion about *Panzerkreuzer oder Brot?* ("Warships or Bread?"). I do not know if she believed that she had convinced or humiliated me by having me read the editorial.

On one of my later visits to Wolfenbüttel, in 1938, I met Fräulein Schmidt in the street, in the middle of the railroad tracks. She stopped me and asked how my parents were doing and added that she never had anticipated that the Nazi regime would follow such an anti-*Jüdische* policy, and that she deeply regretted what was happening to us. I made no comment. While we were facing each other, we heard the warning signals of an approaching train. She bade me good-bye, and we walked off in different directions. When I turned to look after her, I saw her stooped figure slowly gaining distance from me.

When I entered school in 1920, I had been received with a friendly reserve. For a time, I was included in a "chocolate-and-cake circle" called a *Kränzchen*, where we played the piano for each other and gossiped about our teachers. A separation between my classmates became apparent only in later years when Nazi propaganda had raised antisemitism to a new plateau of hatred and the borderline between being accepted and barely tolerated became more visible.

One of the teachers I liked best and had most contact with was Dr. Kössler, our mathematics teacher. Although I was a good student in language arts and history, I had some trouble with algebra. In order to help me catch up to class levels, Dr. Kössler decided to give me tutorials. When I entered his private study for the first time, I was surprised by the pictures hanging on the wall: three of them, depicting the kaiser, Paul von Hindenburg, and E. F. W. Ludendorff, the saints of the monarchists in the Weimar Republic. I had not expected that Dr. Kössler, too, was a follower of the ultraright ideology. During my lessons with him, we had many conversations about politics and Weimar. Before I left Wolfenbüttel, he told me quite openly that he had lost all respect for the Nazi Party when he discovered that, even in his own field, they had twisted the truth and could not be trusted any longer. Like other conservatives, he failed to act on an insight that had come too late.

In his relationship to me, he proved to be helpful and caring. He comforted me when one classmate told me that "I did not belong anymore and that she would no longer speak to me." (In 1986, the former student in question cheerfully let me know that I would be most welcome to join the Alumni Association of the *Schloßschule*. I declined.)

Another significant experience of my time in school was connected with a lesson in religious instruction. Wolfenbüttel is a Protestant town and had to educate its pupils in the Protestant religion. Christian ethics and the early development of the Christian religion were the topics in these lessons conducted by a Protestant pastor, Pastor Clemens. I was the only Jewish girl in the class and was excused from taking part. Most of the time, the class was scheduled for early morning and I could sleep late. But at some point this schedule was changed: the class was inserted in the middle of the school day. It did not make sense for me to go home for such a short time, so I asked Pastor Clemens if I could sit in the back of the classroom and do my homework. He granted my request and promptly forgot about me.

This arrangement worked well for a time, but during one lesson I suddenly became aware that the faces of my classmates were turned toward me, almost on command, and many of them had started to giggle. Then I listened and heard that Pastor Clemens was speaking about Jews and about how in Roman times they had denounced the Christians to their Roman persecutors and that many lives had been lost in the atrocities the Romans visited on the early Christians.

I was stunned and felt my face turn beet red and did not know what to do. I knew immediately that something had to be done to refute this fictitious story and knew also that I must act for myself as well as for my standing in class. Before I had decided what action to take, the moment had passed. Nevertheless, I could not give up trying to rectify this false story. After class I approached Pastor Clemens while he was still at the teacher's desk and without hesitation told him that I had heard what he had been saying about the Jews and their traitorous behavior. I wanted him to know that I, too, had religious instructions: but "in our religion we were taught to respect all religions and not to spread hateful theories about them." Having spoken rather emphatically but without making any accusations, I turned around, shook my black ponytail, walked toward the door, and shut it with a bang.

I knew that I had done something outrageous, even something rebellious, and did not know what the consequences might be. My mother's reaction was one of fear that I might be expelled but our Jewish *Religionslehrer* (religion teacher), Lehrer Steinberg, thought that wrong: my mother should have hugged and kissed me for every word I had said. It did not turn out as she expected, though.

A few days passed. None of the teachers made a remark and I was not cited to appear before Frau Gertrud Hasse.

One or two weeks went by after that incident, and then one day my father received a visitor. He was Konsistorialrat Wicke, a high official of the Protestant Church. I opened the door for him myself and was disquieted by this tall man in black who wore the pastoral collar. He wished to speak with my father. They were closeted for what seemed like a long time. Afterward he left quietly. My father then told us that Mr. Wicke had brought the apologies of Pastor Clemens and his own regrets. He had stressed that such an incident would not happen again.

3

Marriage, Emigration, Divorce: Berlin, Milan, Kladow, 1933–1938

BERLIN ALSO gave me the occasion to take a step in my life that turned out to be unfortunate for me. In 1935, I married an old friend, Wolfram Kahle, whom I had known since my teens—a Christian. At first and for a long time, it was a youthful relationship, with occasional visits between Wolfenbüttel and Berlin, a pleasant pastime during vacations. As a child, I had met his parents, who were friends of my Uncle Ernst and Aunt Hedi. His father had played a role in the Revolution of 1918 that established the Weimar Republic. When I met him, he was the Social Democratic president of Kreuzberg, a borough of Berlin. His wife had studied dentistry and was the first woman dentist in Berlin. Both were Social Democrats and outspoken foes of the Deutsch-Nationale or National-Sozialistische (Nazi) regime. Many of their friends were Jewish. Their son, Wolfram, had inherited their political and social thinking, and his circle of friends, like that of his parents, included many people of diverse background.

Wolfram had started to study law, and had taken the first examination necessary for a judicial career. He had become *Referendar* and had also taken his Dr. iur. As the next prescribed step in this career, he was attached to the Amtsgericht in Beelitz, in the vicinity of Berlin. Soon after the Nazis came to power, the official greeting in every public and government office was changed to "Heil Hitler!" Because Wolfram Kahle was unwilling to say these two words, he gave notice to the Amtsgericht and left: his judicial career had ended. His father died of a heart attack in the early 1930s: I am unable to say if the then prevailing political frictions in Germany were a contributing factor. His mother, a withdrawn and sensitive woman, became unhappy and depressed with the loss of her husband. She committed suicide when her closest friends emigrated to Palestine in 1935.

But, when I moved to Berlin in 1933, my relationship to my Berlin friend changed quickly. He sought my company and took pride in showing me Berlin, its museums and environment. I spent my free time entirely with him: we grew close to each other and married after my two-year apprenticeship came to an end. We left Berlin to build a life in a country that would be free of the taint of Nazism. We went to Milan, Italy, to open a German lending library, but soon discovered that our German Jewish clientele was too small to support us financially. We returned to Berlin when Wolfram was offered a position with my uncle's successor firm, and I took on a secretarial job with a firm selling cameras to prospective emigrants. (Because emigrants were not allowed to own or export currency, they took along expensive German cameras, which they could sell abroad later.) We were lucky to find rooms in a larger apartment in the center of West Berlin that we had to share with the owner.

With time, my expectation of love and steadfastness were disappointed. Shortly after our marriage, I became aware of my husband's unfaithfulness and, worse, he showed disregard and disdain for me. Too late, I discovered that his theories of "free love" and "the culture of nudity" clashed with my beliefs of love and fidelity. I became very unhappy, but carried on with the marriage—which it no longer was—in part because I was ashamed to let my parents know how unhappy I had become. They had warned me of this outcome, but then had accepted Wolfram on my account. However, when he was dismissed from his job for womanizing—harassment in today's language—I could no longer keep up the pretense of happiness. Thus far, I had pushed the idea of separation aside. Now I was so disconsolate that I felt that I could no longer go on living in deepening desperation and dejection and damage to my self-esteem. I could not endure the scenes he made—for no reason—or his criticism of my person and everything I did. Divorce presented itself as the only way out.

It was not easy to go to court and present a case for a non-guilty verdict in a marriage between an "Aryan" and a Jewess.

If I had been declared the guilty party, it would become impossible for me to emigrate: no Western country would have admitted a divorcée in an age when prejudice against divorced women was the accepted pattern. We had to obtain a verdict of non-guilty for the Jewish partner in a marriage with a Christian. Again, the family helped to find an experienced lawyer, and in August 1938, Dr. Wertheim and I had to appear before the Berlin Kammergericht (Berlin Supreme Court). I was asked some rudimentary questions and, after a short conference, the three sitting judges pronounced that I "as a Jewess could not reasonably be expected to continue the marriage any longer." "Es kann ihr als Jüdin nicht länger zugemutet werden, die Ehe aufrecht zu erhalten!" They had pronounced me not guilty! It was an astounding judgment during those Nazi times.

This judgment, passed by a court in Nazi Berlin a few months before Kristallnacht, was quite unusual and against Nazi race doctrine, but it did not affect the sense of failure and inadequacy I suffered from because of this unhappy marriage. After the war, Wolfram applied successfully to the government of the Federal Republic for compensation for the "personal persecution" he had suffered by having been married to a Jewish woman. By then, he had had four more marriages and divorces.

4

The Outbreak of the War, Herbert, Forced Labor: Berlin, 1939–1942

AFTER I HAD LEFT WOLFENBÜTTEL, the conditions for Jews there deteriorated further. How could it be different, with the rowdy SA roaming the streets day and night, yelling slogans of hate "to make Germany *judenrein!*" This acceleration of hatred brought pressure not only on the Jews, but also on the people who had contact with them and who had befriended them for a long time. They were threatened with retaliation if they did not cease their contact. As a result, Jews rapidly felt isolated, unable to pierce the walls of silence and with rejection growing around them.

Finally, in 1937, my parents and my grandmother had the good fortune to leave Wolfenbüttel and move to Kladow, a suburb of Berlin. When my Uncle Ludwig emigrated, he offered them the country house he had built in Kladow on the Wannsee, where I joined them in 1938. We quickly felt at home in Kladow. Uncle Ludwig had bought a piece of lakeshore property and built a house, which served him as a retreat to indulge his hobby—boating on the Wannsee. The house was built in an English country style that fitted well into the landscape without calling attention to itself. A large garden was planned to combine a recreational part with a vegetable garden, all artfully arranged. Low hedges hid the vegetable and strawberry patches from view, and a spacious lawn invited cricket players and offered a wide vista of the Wannsee and the *Pfaueninsel* (Peacock Island).

My mother soon took charge of the household and continued everything she had done in Wolfenbüttel, and my father became an accomplished vegetable gardener. It was an oasis of peace and happiness after the aggression they had suffered in our hometown. Little of the world we left behind penetrated the large hedges that surrounded the property.

Following my divorce, I made an attempt to emigrate to Australia and lost a precious six months waiting for a visa that never came. After this failure, I applied again through the Jüdische Auswanderungsstelle (Jewish Emigration Organization) for permission to emigrate to England and do housework. The visa came in late July 1939. Getting all clearances to obtain a passport to be able to leave Germany took an unconscionably long time: often several weeks, if not months, of waiting.

During this period of delay, our family suffered a loss: my grandmother died in her eighty-ninth year. It was as if her life just gave out; one morning, she did not get up from her bed and barely talked anymore. She died a week later. I know that she hated the Nazis with a passion and used curse words for them. In her eyes, they were responsible for her separation from her sons and the destruction of our family life. We buried her in the Jewish cemetery of Weissensee beside her brother. Two weeks later, the military threat hanging over Europe exploded into World War II. On that day, September 1, 1939, borders around Germany closed, and any hope of leaving Germany withered. We were caught, and the future looked more threatening.

From 1933 to 1938 the central administration for Jews in Germany was the Reichsvertretung der Juden in Deutschland, which had been built up as an independent entity (it was later called Reichsvereinigung). The Jews administered their own school system and established cultural functions and social services as they perceived the need for them, because Berlin was growing into the largest congregation in Germany.

After Hitler came to power, the threat to Jews living in Germany had led to increased emigration, but to many Jews in Germany, the patterns and policies governing emigration were as confusing as a rabbit warren. The Berlin Jüdische Gemeinde had added the Jüdische Auswanderungsstelle to give guidance to the many visa applicants and to direct applications into the right channels, and it helped many hundreds to leave Germany. They also did their best to expedite my emigration, but the war intervened and made it impossible for me to use my permit for England. At the Auswanderungsstelle, I met some of the women officials on a personal basis and befriended them.

At that point, the Jewish Emigration Organization was asked to recruit volunteers for a statistical assignment imposed on the Reichsvereinigung by the Gestapo on short notice. When asked to help with this assignment, I agreed immediately. Other volunteers had come from other Berlin Jewish organizations, including the Lehranstalt für die Wissenschaft des Judentums, the Academy of Jewish Scholarship, the last remaining institute for higher liberal Jewish learning, directed by Rabbi Leo Baeck. One of those who volunteered was Herbert Strauss.

We were directed to a building belonging to the Gemeinde, Joachimsthaler Strasse 13a, and assigned to small groups working both day and night shifts. We were about twenty younger people, men and women. Around midnight, we took a coffee break, a welcome interruption of our work and an occasion to meet each other. The group stayed in existence longer than anticipated and was moved to the day shift to finish the job. By then, the members of the group knew each other well, and friendships had formed.

Sometimes, during these early months of the war, we met on Sunday afternoons in the apartment of one of the volunteers to talk and to listen to music. My new friends also visited me in Kladow on a beautiful October afternoon.

I cannot deny that I was attracted to one of the young men in the group. His name was Herbert Strauss. He was a very silent type and always looked serious. It was intriguing that such a young and good-looking man should be so solitary. His appearance was that of an athlete, and I learned later that this impression was not far from wrong. His face contrasted very much with the rest of his appearance: it was long and thin, with worry lines from nose to mouth and a remote expression. In this way, he created a wall of solitude around himself that said: "Touch me not!"

One afternoon, in the Joachimsthaler Strasse, I was carrying a stack of questionnaires when I realized he was in the room I had entered. He was sitting at a desk, slouched deeply into the chair, and wearing knicks (knickerbockers). His *Haferlschuhe* (a type of tasseled brogues) were sticking out from under the desk. He was scrutinizing a document he held in his hands and did not look up when I entered or when I crossed the room. Before leaving through the other door, I halted, thinking that somebody should really make an attempt to prick this balloon of solitude. Why not me? No sooner thought than done: in holding the door open for my exit, I turned to him and asked, "Don't you *ever* smile?" ("Ja, lachen Sie denn *niemals*?") With that, I closed the door behind me, leaving him with my little barb and wondering if it had hit. It had! A week later, he called me to invite me to his room for an afternoon of tea and cake. While I was still pondering the invitation, he shot a barb of his own: "Are you afraid?" Of course, after that I accepted immediately, not telling him that, indeed, I was fearful of not keeping the rule of "no-no to boy and girl alone in a room," not so much for my own reputation, but for the impression my immediate acceptance would make on him. But, then, I also wanted to be lighthearted to see if I could coax this young man out of the sullens. My expectation of finding a withdrawn young man was completely misplaced. When he opened the door for me and led me to his room, I could not have been more surprised. He had neatly arranged a little table with tea for two: a small vase with flowers in the middle, a tray with sweets, and my favorite cake. I could not believe that he had noticed during our coffee breaks that I liked *Pflaumenkuchen* (plum cake). I had thought that he was hardly aware of his surroundings and that such mundane observances were beneath him. Why had he suddenly changed? I looked at him questioningly, and then—for the first time—I saw his smile. It started at his mouth and then ran like a little ripple upward until it had reached his eyes, and there it rested, maybe not quite innocently because he had seen my astonishment and looked at me quizzically. In a split second, it dawned on me that I had misjudged him and that this silent observer had come alive with a suddenness that startled me. Here, beside me, was a young man of flesh and blood who showed that he found me attractive and was drawn to me. His expression had an immediate effect on me: I was in a state of animation, floating on air, and I had to hold on to myself to prevent my joyful exuberance from welling over. I could not well let him know that I responded in kind on the spot and in the first few minutes of our meeting, I started to tease him, and another side of him appeared: his repartees were whimsical. Teatime was filled with banter, one trying to outdo the other. We laughed with each other and were in high spirits.

When we turned to a more serious topic, I learned the reason for his remote behavior: he, too, had received an emigration permit for England, but his passport was handed to him on one of the first days of the war, September 3, 1939. With the passport in his pocket, he had seen the English embassy leave Berlin on that day, but he had made an attempt to leave Germany with a group of other permit holders via the Netherlands the next day. The Dutch police had told them that the border had been closed and that their visas were no longer valid. He also referred to "a girl who was waiting in England." In a few days, or hours, his plans for the future had gone awry. He spoke in a matter-of-fact voice, but I understood what it meant for him: to lose a future in a free country, to face hatred and antagonism instead, with no way out.

Though I left him in a more serious mood, the echo of our meeting lived in both of us, and it seemed natural that we would meet again soon. Herbert came to Kladow, and together we took long walks along the lake through the pinetree country of the Mark Brandenburg, enjoying its melancholy mood, as Leistikow had painted it. Walking was the easiest way for Herbert to talk freely about his thoughts and his concerns. The totalitarian state had taught him to isolate himself, and he had turned to poetry, literature, and history. He looked inward to his own development: his religion, his relationship to others and to women, and, last but not least, his professional goals and his service to the community. The last question touched on his studies at the Lehranstalt für die Wissenschaft des Judentums. (During the High Holidays in the fall of 1941, Herbert was asked to direct religious services and give sermons in a Gemeinde as a *Hilfs-Rabbiner*, an assistant rabbi. Later, he asked himself if he should volunteer to join a deportation transport and help as much as possible. Leo Baeck and I dissuaded him.)

As Herbert told me later, he was also taken by my direct, feminine way of simplifying issues that appeared complex to him. With astonishment, I realized that his values differed from mine and that he lived a life based on those values. I understood what he wanted to do with his life and wished to share in it; I had made this decision on first sight. I knew that it would not be simple, but I was aware of my strong emotions and wanted to give him as much tenderness as I could find in myself.

At the time, Herbert met my parents in Kladow but they had received him with reserve. My mother worried for me and wished that I would find a stable and protective companion and not a longtime friendship. (How Herbert and I have wished for our sake and hers that her attitude had been different—if only she could have known the future.)

I did not follow the advice of my mother to end the friendship with Herbert; on the contrary, we moved closer to each other. We continued our walks even during the cold spells of this first *Kriegswinter*, when the Wannsee was frozen over. We walked on solid ice to the *Pfaueninsel*, which added adventure to it. Much of what we talked about was new to me. During the summer, we swam from the pier. Herbert was a powerful swimmer and enjoyed diving into the water and taking long-distance swims. We acquired a little canoe and discovered the green inlets of the Havel lakes in the vicinity of Kladow. We had to give up these excursions when the canoe sprang a leak.

The events of the war brought us closer together. Hitler's surprise attack on Poland filled us with loathing. It revealed his murderous war plans to gain *Lebensraum* in the East and to team up with the Soviet Union. What were his ultimate war aims? Could Hitler be beaten back by the French and English armies? Remembering his deviousness, I felt a loathing and constriction in myself that made me recoil when in April 1940 he attacked Denmark and Norway, and on May 10 marched his armies into neutral Holland and Belgium, overwhelming them in a matter of days. His Luftwaffe reduced Rotterdam to ruins; he defeated France and occupied Paris. We watched it with rising apprehension.

The "realists" among us had always assumed that ultranationalist Germany had planned for the domination of Europe. But that Hitler would extend his power over Western Europe and turn its states into vassals was a disaster of a magnitude we had not believed possible. Our hopes of being freed of this monster were dashed. We had to postpone our hopes yet again. Herbert and I drew closer to comfort each other and lived through a time that sometimes seemed beyond endurance as Germany won victories on land and at sea. Hitler's hoarse threats against us and all European Jewry took on an ever more sinister plausibility.

A new chapter in this bloody story began on June 22, 1941, when Hitler launched his attack on the Soviet Union. It came as a total surprise to us because the two countries had just concluded a nonaggression treaty and seemed to be getting along with each other, dividing the spoils.

On that Sunday afternoon, Herbert and I were on our way from Kladow into town. In Pichelsdorf, we boarded a crowded tramway. *Sondermeldungen*, extra military bulletins, had trumpeted the news: everybody knew. People talked to each other, but I thought that they were rather subdued. Herbert and I could barely hide our excitement and, with an effort, kept silent. We knew of each other's emotion, and even today we recall our feelings on that particular afternoon and use the same expressions to speak of it. Those people in the streetcar: were they so sure of victory, another conquest to add to their win-column? Had they no feeling for the deaths another military attack would bring to an innocent people? On that sunny afternoon in June, with voices buzzing around us, we felt that history had turned a new page, and a new and different chapter would be written.

It would also be the last chapter of Jewish life in Germany. Since the beginning of the war in 1939, our living space had become more and more restricted. The Nazis created a new body of *Judengesetze* (special antisemitic legislation) and were steadily adding and inventing new ones: a *Kennkarte* (identity card for Jews) with the letter "J" stamped on it; women had to use the name Sara as an additional first name, men the name Israel. It was another way of excluding and humiliating Jews. To harass us, an 8:00 P.M. curfew was imposed on us, and the use of public transportation was also restricted. We were issued special rationing cards, and shopping hours were shortened to an hour and a half at the end of regular store hours. My family was not as badly off as many others: my mother had seen to it that friendly contacts did not lapse when the new stringent laws were introduced, and fruits, vegetables, and even flowers from the garden made it possible to return some of the favors we received. I did what I could to share some of the surplus with Herbert: cooking a warm meal for him was something I liked to do, and we felt like celebrating our togetherness during these hard times.

At one time, during the war, our telephones were requisitioned, and we had to hand over our household silver. My mother and I decided, in a gesture of defiance, to bury part of the silver in the garden. Later, in 1958, when you were eleven years old, Janie, we took our first European trip from New York and visited Kladow. We had not told you of what had happened to us in Germany. Who would have wanted to burden a child with the horrors of Nazi times? I indicated to Herbert where to dig for the silver in the garden: when his shovel made a metallic sound, you thought that we were on a treasure hunt and you were delighted with our find: the silver cups and bread basket that Herbert dug up that day now stand on a shelf in your home. Unfailingly, they are a reminder of my mother and of a past that will always be with us.

One of the most degrading of the Nazis' sick measures goes back to September 19, 1941, when—three months after the invasion of Russia—the Nazis ordered Jews to wear the *Judenstern*, the Jewish star, made of yellow cloth with the hebraized word *Jude* on it. It was to be worn on all outer garments, on the left side near the heart. A day after this new law came into force, five young Jews—among them Herbert and his friend Ernst Ludwig Ehrlich, "Lutz"—walked down the Kurfürstendamm provocatively wearing the star. The *Völkische Beobachter* (the newspaper of propaganda minister Goebbels) commented that Jewish conceit like this demonstration would soon be eradicated. Now Jews were marked, expected to cringe.

As one law followed the other, the burden became ever more oppressive and the severity harder to bear. The latest new law was of far-reaching consequences for every German Jew, including Herbert and me. This law decreed that all able Jews had to be drafted for work. It meant forced labor in war factories under difficult and discriminatory conditions. A few months after the decree was issued (summer 1941), I received a notice from the Gemeinde to come to a meeting in the Joachimsthaler Strasse.

Again, as in September 1939, a large group had assembled. The president of the Gemeinde informed us that it would be advisable to volunteer for work because it might protect us against "deportation." There! We heard it for the first time, officially, that dreaded word *deportation*! I heeded the advice and soon after was "lucky" to find work in a factory that made radios for war planes.

At the time I was drafted for "forced labor," Herbert was still deferred as a student of the Lehranstalt für die Wissenschaft des Judentums, but a short time later he received a summons from the *Arbeitsamt* (the labor exchange for Jews): its director had the reputation of being an outspoken antisemite. Apparently, as a person and especially as a young Jewish intellectual, Herbert raised the man's ire and spitefulness, so as a punishment for being what he was, he was sent to the Strassendepot Lankwitz to do the least respected work possible: cleaning the streets of a southern suburb of Berlin.

5

The Deportation of My Parents, Flight from the Gestapo: Berlin, October 24, 1942

THE FACTORY that employed me was called Funktechnische Werkstätten Nikolaus and was located in Berlin at the Köpenicker Strasse 156. The owner was Horst Parlo. He employed approximately one hundred people, manufacturing radios for airplanes. The little group of four I was attached to worked with copper bobbins that had to be plated with a special tin alloy. Because I could not reach my work place from Kladow in time for the morning shift, we decided that I should take a room in Charlottenburg in the midwestern part of Berlin. From there I could reach the factory in approximately one hour by Stadtbahn (elevated subway) from the Charlottenburg Station; it also had the advantage of being closer to Herbert.

It was relatively simple to find a furnished room, because all Jewish apartment owners were forced to rent out their empty or unused rooms. My first residence was in the Mommsenstrasse with a retired Justizrat, a judicial officer formerly attached to the Department of Justice. His name was Mattersdorf; and he looked like the subject of a painting by El Greco. He must have been in his late seventies, had a long face and bushy gray eyebrows, and gave the impression of being an old and dignified gentleman. When he spoke to me, he was always sitting in a chair, a blanket neatly folded over his knees, his cane lying on top of it, with his hands folded on it. He, thus, gave a rigid impression, but he was soft-spoken and even friendly. One day he informed me in his even tones that he had to ask me to move out, because he had gotten his deportation orders: he almost pleaded for my understanding. I was near tears. During this interview, his housekeeper stood beside him; she was a statuesque "Aryan" woman from East Prussia with ruddy cheeks, her hair pulled straight back. She wore a light-blue uniform and a white apron with a big bow. She had a steady expression, and it was my impression that she treated Mr. Mattersdorf with slightly bossy friendliness. As I remember the scene now, it could have been a painting by a Dutch genre painter, entitled *Master and Servant*. But the most significant aspect of this scene was Justizrat Mattersdorf's belief that the Deutsche Rechtsstaat could not be destroyed by the Nazis, even by his own death. A *Gedenkbuch* (memorial volume)* issued by the German Bundesarchiv in Koblenz lists Justizrat Mattersdorf as having been deported to Theresienstadt, the ghetto for the privileged and old people, and reports that he had died there. He belonged to a generation that believed in government as honorable; to him it was incomprehensible that innocent fellow men could be destroyed out of sheer hatred.

After I had to give up the room with Justizrat Mattersdorf in Mommsenstrasse, I found another in the same area, in the Niebuhrstrasse, just around the corner from Schlüterstrasse, where Herbert lived.

I could not foresee then how quickly that dangerous situation would threaten my parents and me. Most weekends I spent in Kladow with my parents. One weekend in September 1942, after I had worked almost a year at the factory, my mother told me that my uncle's real estate agent, Mr. Schürmann, and his assistant, Mr. Schmidt, had come with a *Ritterkreuzträger*, a highly decorated German Luftwaffe officer, with the intention of taking over the Kladow house. We feared that we would be dispossessed by the officer and decided that my parents should move out as quickly as possible.

Our moving out did not solve our problems, however. Only three weeks later, my father received notice from the Berlin Jüdische Gemeinde that he would be "resettled in the East." We were not sure whether the resettlement order was meant only for my father. In a previous transport, they had taken only men, at least from some groups they wanted to punish with special

---

*An official publication listing all Jewish dead in the *Konzentrationslager: Opfer der Verfolgung der Juden unter Nationalsozialistischer Gewaltherrschaft in Deutschland, 1933–1945*.

severity. Would my mother let him go alone? Though I hoped to save at least one of my parents, it didn't seem possible. I went to see them in their new "home" in the Mecklenburgische Allee to discuss what could be done to avoid the fateful situation. When I entered, my father was sitting at a table with dozens of family photos spread out in front of him. He stared at a picture of my brother wearing the uniform of the British police in Palestine. Tears were running down his cheeks. I spent many hours trying to persuade my parents to disobey the order and to hide underground in Berlin. Such action would have presented very difficult problems, because they had lived for years in the semirural environment of Kladow and knew only a few Christian friends in town who might or might not have been willing to hide them. In Kladow they would have been recognized immediately. My father would not consider the idea seriously. He had spent all his life as an honored citizen of our town, Wolfenbüttel, and had held several honorary positions, supervising local elections and similar activities. He also had taken an active role in a local veterans' organization along with my mother's uncle, a founder of the organization and a decorated war hero of 1866 and 1870. My father could not conceive of acting against authority himself. He was sixty years old. For me it was the most heartbreaking situation: could at least one of them be spared for now? But my mother would not let my father go alone. I spent the night with them.

My mother returned letters I had written home through the years, the ordinary letters a young person writes home. But there were others that dealt with my feelings toward my mother, to whom I felt very close. She had collected them and handed them to me neatly bundled, with a ribbon tied around them. I was surprised by her gesture: I suddenly understood more than before what a self-disciplined person she was, subduing her emotions even at this moment of separation and giving up these tokens of my love for her, which must have been very dear to her.

My mother and I separated at the door. We did not dare to speak, lest our feelings overwhelm us. We hugged each other and then stepped away to look at one another. I cannot understand to this day why at that moment our self-control did not break down. I never forgot her last look at me and the feelings expressed in her eyes: there were worries in her eyes, but I knew later that she took me in to keep the memory of me for the rest of her life. How I looked I do not know, but I could not leave without touching her. I caressed her cheek—it felt cool and tender—and the memory of my touching her is still with me to this day. I then turned away from her and walked down the steps to the garden and into the street. I did not leave; I wanted to be there, at least in the distance until the Gestapo came to pick them up. I walked along the hedges, up and down the deserted street, and up and down again. I watched the northern gray sky with low-hanging clouds driven by a cold wind. It was a heavy leaden sky, full with rain. I wished and hoped that "they" would not come to take my parents, but I knew that there was no hope. I was distraught. Where was God? There was no answer from the sky and no hope in my heart.

Slowly it grew dark, and I could not survey the surrounding area any longer. What I would have done if the Gestapo had come during the daylight hours and driven my parents off or marched off with them, I am unable to say. Reluctantly, I left the scene in the Mecklenburgische Allee and went to Schlüterstrasse to see if Herbert had returned from work. I was concerned about him, too, because he had been given a different assignment the day before. He was not home when I arrived, and that was a new worry. Every change in the daily routine could mean danger. In my distress, I took his absence as a bad omen and felt anxious about his safety. Just a few days earlier, friends of ours had gone into hiding and had to leave their luggage with one of us until they had found a more permanent hiding place. Herbert had gladly agreed to have it stored in his room, and this became a new problem for me. If Herbert had an encounter with the Gestapo and if that luggage was detected in his room, it could lead to further complications for him, so I started to bring it all to my room. I had to make several trips because there was a suitcase, some bags, and a knapsack.

After I moved the luggage in my room, I went back to the Schlüterstrasse and waited for him to come home, thinking about my parents and their fate. I did not know what had happened to them, and I had no way to find out anything. I waited in desperation, not knowing when fate would strike: against my parents, against Herbert, against me, against all those who were close to me.

It was almost 8 o'clock—the curfew time for Jews living in Berlin. I could not risk waiting much longer. In the areas where we were known, we wore the *Judenstern* as the Nazis had prescribed. To be seen without it and be recognized could mean deportation. To be seen with it after curfew time was equally dangerous. Therefore, I left shortly past the curfew time and went back to my room, which was just around the corner.

Niebuhrstrasse 76, third floor, was the place where my room was located. It was a large apartment and belonged to Mrs. Elisa Lentz and her daughter. There were four or five other tenants, whom I had met briefly. I had not been there for long, and they were as busy with work and survival as I was. The one exception was Dr. Ilse Kassel, who occupied the room opposite mine. We had met and liked each other, and she entrusted me with "her story." She was a physician and came from a family of doctors. Her father had been a practicing physician in the northern part of Berlin, where all the big factories were located, and most of his patients were workers or trade unionists, sympathetic to radical, left causes. She had inherited her father's practice and with it the dedication—characteristic for many German Jewish doctors—to care for the workers and the underprivileged. No wonder they were the butt of Nazi aggression. What she had to go through was heartbreaking.

On April 1, 1933, the day of the Nazi decreed *Judenboykott* throughout Germany, uniformed SA men blocked her door to prevent patients from entering. A short time later, her right to treat insurance patients was withdrawn by the government. A year later, she was arrested on the allegation of having performed abortions. After she had spent more than a year in detention, a jury declared her innocent. In short succession, she was arrested again and accused of belonging to the Communist resistance movement. She was convicted of very minor offenses and sentenced to three years of hard labor. The court in sentencing her claimed that she, as a Jewish person, should have shown special restraint.

When she was released from prison in 1941, Germany was in

the middle of the war, and the deportations of Jews to the East had already begun. Because of her conviction for high treason, the Friedrich Wilhelm Universität in Berlin revoked her medical license. For a short time, she was able to work as a nurse in a Jewish hospital in Berlin-Wedding, but then was forced to work in an armament factory for a mere pittance. When her mother's monthly allowance from Israel was appropriated by the Nazi regime, she and her daughter became destitute and needed to be supported by relatives. A brief respite from financial worries came when a former patient of hers offered to take the two of them in on a farm she owned near Berlin. But fate was inexorable. In the fall of 1943, the hiding place was betrayed, and Ilse Kassel committed suicide before the Gestapo arrived. Her six-year-old daughter was sent to Auschwitz. The address in Niebuhrstrasse served as her legal address only; her friends had found a hiding place for her, because she was more in peril of being deported than other Jews were. It was a miracle that she had not been shipped to the East directly from prison.

That evening, when I returned to Niebuhrstrasse, Dr. Kassel was not home. I had so wished for a word with her, but again I was alone with my worries about my parents. I saw them before me in their helplessness, overwhelmed by an inhuman fate they could not fight. My desperation at not being able to help them hit me repeatedly, and was growing. Like a stone that keeps rolling back, it came crashing down. I blamed myself for not having had enough foresight, for selfishness, for an attitude of unjustified optimism in a life-threatening situation. They were certainly lost! It was a burden placed on me that has remained unbearably hard to live with.

My worries about Herbert's whereabouts also intensified. Where was he? I waited another hour for him—wishing, hoping, that he would come and tell me that he had arrived home safely. But this hope was disappointed. When I realized that I would not see him that evening, I prepared for the night and went to bed.

I was in a deep sleep when I heard, dreamlike, a ringing bell. The sound was slowly beginning to penetrate my awareness when, suddenly, I was jolted from sleep and startled to see Miss Lentz opening the door and two men behind her. Sitting up, I noticed that the time was 3:30 A.M. As the men entered my room, they identified themselves as *Geheime Staatspolizei* (Secret Police), then gave my name, and when and where I was born. They had it right; I nodded. The voice at that point was not particularly harsh—not until later—but I needed no external sign of their power to know the threatening situation I was in. Watching them, I felt a curious detachment: young men at the end of their twenties in tweed jackets and felt hats with chamois tufts. Their SS uniform jodhpurs, heavy jackboots, and guns in leather holsters were signs of their military affiliation. They were young German men with a death-dealing occupation.

They ordered me to get up. I slipped on my morning gown, which was on a chair nearby. One of them opened the conversation by telling me that they had orders to take me to Levetzowstrasse—the *Sammelpunkt* (collection point) for all deportations from Berlin—"where they had taken my parents before," and he added, almost cheerfully, "that they were sure that I wanted to be with them." I was standing before the two men and felt a heaviness rising in me and my knees buckling, so that I had to hold on to a dresser in order not to fall. The curtain behind which so many of my friends, and now my parents, had disappeared was opening for me, and I would soon know what terrible secrets it hid. But before yielding to this fate, I wanted to make an attempt to extricate myself from it, and in doing so I made a terrible mistake. My strong attachment to Herbert and my unwillingness to separate from him led me to say that I had a half-Jewish boyfriend. "Oh," the Gestapo man responded. "Who is he?" While I was still speaking, I realized that I had tricked myself with a false hope and that I had acted irresponsibly, putting Herbert in jeopardy, without helping myself at all. My own feelings had betrayed me. I knew my fate was decided, but I could not allow Herbert to share it with me, or I would feel a traitor for the rest of my life. Quickly, I tried to recover and named a friend—the son of my deported friends the Herzenbergs—who had emigrated to Australia in 1937. One of the men, the self-appointed "speaker," asked me for his address, and I gave it to him with the safe knowledge that he was in Melbourne, Australia, and his parents had been deported to Litzmannstadt in Poland a year before. (Earlier, I had been informed that Mr. Herzenberg had "died" in the ghetto of Litzmannstadt-Lodz.) Nothing I said could have worsened their fate.

The next moment brought new difficulties. They discovered the luggage belonging to our friends, which I had stored in my room that very evening. Suddenly, it aroused their curiosity. The speaker asked me about it, and, without waiting for my answer, he took a bag and the knapsack and emptied the contents on my bed: it was a helter-skelter pile of heavy sweaters and other bad weather gear. I was not sure that the Gestapo realized that these belongings had been packed for the purpose of hiding and surviving in hard conditions. They became quite suspicious, and the speaker's tone of voice was unmistakably threatening when he asked me a second time who the owner of these items was. I was startled by that question, because I could not give the name of the friends without endangering them further. I answered, as coolly as I could, that they belonged to my parents and me and were taken with us when we were forced to leave the house in Kladow in great haste.

The speaker told me with a sneer: "Nobody has ever lied to me on an empty stomach [*nüchternen Magen*] as you have just done."

He was looking at me with ironic contempt. How could I have the audacity to lie to him? He, the exponent of Hitler's victorious Germany, which had decreed the end of Judaism. He, who could step on me and crush me or shoot me, make an end of me whichever way he liked. Here I was behaving as if I had rights that I was not willing to relinquish—not even in this threatening situation. He was not used to being defied: Jews had to obey and to acquiesce in a life without dignity, without rights, and, finally, in their own deaths. He knew the system of destruction Hitler and Himmler had created, and he, the Gestapo man in my room, and his cohorts on the streets were getting victims for this machine as quickly and as efficiently as possible. He knew that I could not outrun the turning wheel. He was here to make sure that I was caught in its spokes. Finally, he took his contemptuous eyes off me and directed his attention again to the luggage. Among it was a suitcase with the initials C. B. Again he asked me to identify its owner. This question put me into a tight corner because I just could not give him the name of the owner, our friend Carl Bielschowski, without delivering him, his mother, and sister—who had all worked with me—into the hands of the Gestapo. Would the Gestapo conduct a special search for them? No, I could not risk that. My quandary grew: I could not name just anybody, or invent any name. It had to be a real person, but one who was safely out of the clutches of the Gestapo. How long it took me to come up with a name, I cannot remember, but finally I gave them the name of an uncle of mine, Carl Bildesheim, who had emigrated to Argentina. The Gestapo man growled at me, knowing that I had lied again. He then asked me for the key to the suitcase and I had to tell him that it was not in my possession. I felt my anxiety rising; I was trembling, anticipating the next question: "Who has it?" I did not know where to turn; all ways seemed to be barred. My imagination stymied. And then in my desperation I named my father, which has left me with guilt feelings to this day. I do not know in what measurable or immeasurable way I had added to the terrible fate of my parents. Not only that, what about the Bielschowskis—what would happen to them after this night? Would they also disappear behind the curtain that existed only in my imagination? (Yes, they did: in Switzerland in 1945, at the Tiefenau Hospital near Bern, I learned from a Czech physician—Dr. Hadras—that Carl Bielschowski had been deported to Auschwitz and his mother and sister sent to Theresienstadt and from there to Auschwitz.)

After realizing that there was no way to open that suitcase now other than by forcing it, they turned toward me and ordered me to dress and pack a small suitcase. They demanded that I be ready in ten minutes. Then they withdrew from my room. I dressed and started to make an effort to pack a suitcase. But at that moment I lost my resolve. I did not know what to do next: I could not focus on anything clearly. Finally, I found a suitcase, but I did not know what to put in it. I walked around unthinkingly, fastening on the thought that I had five minutes, only five minutes, to make reasonable choices about what to take on a trip in a cattle car to a *Konzentrationslager*—concentration camp—in the East in near wintry conditions. Yes, I would have to take all the warm things I had. Only then did I think of the heavy coat that a tailor had made for me at my mother's insistence for just such an eventuality. It did not have the Jewish star on it, because I had not worn it yet. What was I to do? I decided that I would ask the secret policemen if somebody among the women in the apartment could sew the star on for me. I stepped into the corridor and saw that the door to the room opposite mine, Dr. Kassel's room, was wide open, and that the two Gestapo men were in there searching it. (Somebody absent during curfew time was always suspect.) I stepped into her room and saw them crouching and bending over some of her belongings. When I asked my question, I realized that they were in the farthest corners of the room and could not see my door or the entrance hallway from where they were. It came like a lightning decision to me—almost without my participation—"Away! Away!" I asked my question and they answered in the affirmative. From that moment on, I acted without thinking. I turned on my heels, took the few steps back to my room, mechanically dropped the coat on a chair, put on my regular coat, took my pocketbook, made sure that Herbert's house key was in it, tiptoed through the hallway past another room where a frightened old woman saw me but did not understand what was going on.

I reached the entrance door of the apartment, opened it slowly, and stepped outside, leaving the door ajar, and started to walk down the carpeted stairwell as quietly as I could. I tried to listen behind me to determine if anybody had noticed my passing by, but everything was quiet. It seemed a long time before I finally reached the house door, which I carefully opened to survey the dark street scene. I noticed the parked police car, mounted with a blue light. I had no choice but to pass it. Luckily there was no driver in the car, and the two secret policemen were upstairs. I passed the car and rounded the corner into Schlüterstrasse. At the same time, I loosened the stitches of the Jewish star sewn on my coat and removed it. Slowly my panic subsided and reason returned. I knew very well what I must do: warn Herbert. I opened the house door of Schlüterstrasse 53 with my key, walked as quickly as I could, trying not to make much noise, through the front entrance into the yard of the Gartenhaus, and climbed the three flights to the apartment where he lived. I pressed the bell in our long-adopted sign—the rhythm of the first five notes of Beethoven's Fifth Symphony, which was also Churchill's famous sign for victory. Nobody opened the door. I simply could not understand it. Mrs. Neumann, Herbert's landlady, and her companion must be home, and Herbert, too, assuming that he had come home during the evening hours. Were they too frightened to open the door? I was desperate, because I knew that I had a lead of only minutes until the Gestapo found out where I had gone. Everybody in my place knew that Herbert and I were close friends. I knew that the Gestapo would soon be following me, that it would take only a short time to find out Herbert's name and address. My fear was that Herbert, in this way, would be drawn into the Gestapo net on account of me: this must not happen! I must not allow it to happen! I waited and waited for somebody to answer: time seemed interminable. Where was I to turn in my anxiety? To let more time elapse without establishing contact seemed senseless. Had I escaped the Gestapo in vain: were they now to get two victims instead of one? Was there nothing I could do to avoid this situation? There must be a way! Finally, in trepidation, I turned away from this door, through which I had stepped so many times before with the happy expectation of meeting Herbert. At that crucial moment, it was locked. Slowly, I walked down three flights, making as little noise as possible. Every neighbor was a possible danger.

Once I reached the street, I ran and ran as fast as I could to the Lietzenburgerstrasse post office, and from a telephone booth in the street, I phoned Christl Simon, our "safe Aryan person." On her last visit from Lausanne, Switzerland, my Aunt Ilse Schöneberg had given me Christl Simon's name, address, and telephone number to use in an emergency, "only in an emergency!" This was an emergency, but Christl Simon thought that her involvement would only endanger Herbert and herself, and the situation then would get completely out of hand: for Herbert, for me, and for herself. Aid given by Christians to help Jewish persons was severely punished, and helping me might also put in jeopardy the Jewish woman she was hiding in her apartment at Fehrbelliner Platz.

I understood her refusal to help me, because she would not be able to warn Herbert of the danger he was in. I had to return to Schlüterstrasse and try again to rouse him in his apartment.

As fast as I could, I ran back to Schlüterstrasse, and this time

Mrs. Neumann opened the door for me. Without waiting for my story, she told me that she had recognized me at my first attempt as I was leaving the courtyard. She then woke Herbert and told him of my attempt to make contact with him and of my departure when nobody had opened the door. Herbert then went to my apartment to see what had happened. As I listened to her words, I felt sheer terror for the second time that night. I could not absorb what she told me: it was the worst message she could have given me. My heart was stricken. I said that I would go back and give myself up to the Gestapo, because I knew Herbert must have run straight into the trap that I had escaped a short time ago. "No, do not do that," was Mrs. Neumann's advice. Herbert had been back to report that he had found the apartment door open, heard the loud voices of the Gestapo, and also seen some of the tenants huddled in the hallway of the apartment, but had not seen me among them.

A short time later, he had left again to watch what was going on from the darkened entrance of one of the buildings opposite mine. "That is where he probably is right this minute," she said. As briefly as I could, I told her what had happened to me and left, anxious to find Herbert. I looked into one of the dark entrances where he had said he would be, but had no luck.

I was very careful and moved around as much as possible along the shadows of the buildings in the dark, and tried to avoid the bluish parking lights of the Gestapo car that was still parked before my apartment building in the Niebuhrstrasse. I was confused about the time, but I knew that the minutes for our escape were running out. I moved away from Herbert's apartment toward the elevated subway at Savignyplatz. The clock showed 5:30 A.M., exactly two hours after the Gestapo had entered my room.

It was the night of October 24, 1942. The dark surrounded me, and I felt terribly lonely and abandoned. If only I could find Herbert, if only I could run toward him, I would be rid of this feverish anxiety that had taken hold of me. I knew that I must suppress my panic and that I must be as quiet as the stillness of this night. I stood silently, looking toward the big station clock, watching the minute hand of the big clock move with a little jerk to the next minute, to the next, and to the next, feeling with every little jump that the time was chasing me—us—that it was heedless of our fate. While I was standing motionless, I had only one thought, which I repeated and repeated like a litany: "Please let me find him, please let me find him!" Later I knew it was a prayer.

Herbert, too, must have realized that we both were in immediate danger of being caught for deportation, of our lives ending in a *Konzentrationslager*. He had been told by Mrs. Neumann that I had tried to contact him in the middle of the night; he had seen the Gestapo in my apartment. He was now trying to find me in the dark streets of the neighborhood and did not know where to look. There was no question in my mind that we must get out of the clutches of the Gestapo and find a place to hide. I was sure that Herbert would feel the same way. We had talked before about the eventuality of hiding, though never anticipating how exactly we could accomplish it. So far, we both had felt reasonably secure because we were working. Mr. Parlo, the owner of the factory where I worked and a well-meaning man, had already warned me, though, that working in an armament factory might not keep Jews safe in the future.

All these considerations swept through my mind in rapid succession while I was still standing in the entrance of Bahnhof Savignyplatz. What was I to do? What must I do? It became clear to me that I must make a third attempt to meet Herbert as soon as I could. Since I was last in his apartment, at least twenty minutes had elapsed. Herbert, too, would have realized that we could not find each other in the darkened streets. To wait longer was to lose the lead we had before. Also, daylight was not more than one hour away. We had to act fast.

Again I had to force myself not to run, but walked at a steady pace the short distance toward Schlüterstrasse 53. Again I entered the front entrance of the building with my own key and then moved as quietly as I could through the front hallway, where the superintendent, Mr. Carlsson, had his apartment. Under no circumstances was he to be alerted to the comings-and-goings of this night. Then I walked equally carefully along the courtyard toward the entrance of the side wing, leading to Mrs. Neumann's apartment on the third floor. I climbed the steps as quietly as I could to avoid any unnecessary noise—a suspicious neighbor and the game would be up. Finally, I ar-

rived at the third-floor landing and rang the bell in our prearranged rhythm, and this time Herbert opened the door. He wore
a coat and carried a small knapsack: he was ready to leave. His
face smiling, he looked happy. "Wonderful, how you got away,"
and with that, he spontaneously opened his arms as if to welcome me and I took a step and was in his arms for one short
moment, leaning my head against his shoulder. With his presence, I had forgotten all anxiety and wished that I could rest
there. But Herbert would not delay for one moment, so I entered
his room to take an envelope with money and an address that
my mother had given me to use in an emergency, both of which
I had hidden in Herbert's room. Then I joined him at the entrance door, and we started to walk down the staircase on tiptoe.
When we reached the first-floor landing, the hallway light went
out, and we continued to descend in darkness, Herbert reaching
out to guide me.

When we came to the last steps, we heard the voice of Mr.
Carlsson, the superintendent of the building. Almost immediately there were other voices and hammering fists on the front
door: "Gestapo, Gestapo, open the door!" We were caught! By
then we were standing in the courtyard, trapped! "Too late, too
late" was my sinking feeling. Why had I run? Now, they had
two victims instead of only one! Suddenly, I felt Herbert's hand
on my wrist in a hard grip. He pulled me away from the staircase
and forward across the backyard, where steps led down to the
air raid shelter. In all this anxiety, we must have moved fast and
silently. We were still descending the stairs to the shelter when
we heard the sound of the heavy jackboots of the Gestapo in the
courtyard and moments later up the staircase to Mrs. Neumann's apartment. Was it possible? Had they seen us? No, they
had not! Nobody was following us! It was still dark. Had Mr.
Carlsson observed us before and had he delayed the opening of
the entrance door for the fraction of time we needed to gain the
security of the shelter? We did not know. Were we safe? Would
Mr. Carlsson keep silent? Or would the two Gestapo men inter-
rogate and threaten Mrs. Neumann and find out that we had left
only minutes before? We did not know. We did not talk, or even
whisper. I followed Herbert to the back of the air raid shelter,
which was furnished with bunk beds. I climbed up and hid my
body as well as I could, pressing it as flat as possible against the

sack cloth, my head down, not wishing to hear or see anything but just knowing that Herbert was close by. The time we spent like this seemed unconscionably long, but we had to remain shrouded by the shadows of the shelter as long as possible. Suddenly, we heard the racket of their boots in the stairwell: they were coming down. Would they come? Had they found out about us? We heard them marching across the yard and the heavy front door falling shut, then silence. They had left! I was still too stunned to trust our luck. In this moment of hesitation and doubt, Herbert said, "I will go up and see what they have done." "No, no," I whispered and tried to hold him back. He was already on his way up. I just could not take any more stress. Sitting on a lower bunk, I covered my face with my hands and started crying, then sobbing. I was so terror stricken that I could not control the agitation that shook me from within. After what seemed like a long time, I became calmer, then I cradled myself, burying my head in my crossed arms. I could not forgive Herbert for—as I believed—getting himself into new danger and leaving me when I was so frightened and distressed. I don't think that he realized the agonizing minutes I would go through during his absence. When he returned, he reported that the Gestapo had not concerned themselves with Mrs. Neumann, which I heard with a sigh of relief. (She had overheard their first remark, though, when they realized that Herbert was not at home, "Ah, the bird [Strauss means 'ostrich'] has flown the nest.") Apparently, they searched his room, and we never knew if they had taken anything. They then sealed the room and left.

Now we were free to leave the shelter. Wary of the stillness around us, we tiptoed up the stone stairs of the cellar entrance and then crossed the yard, toward the front door. I did not see Mr. Carlsson, but Herbert said that he waved to him. We came up to the front door. Herbert opened it carefully to see if the Gestapo car might be parked in front of the building. Everything seemed clear. It was only when we walked out into the street that we realized that it had become day, the October sun shining brightly. It seemed to me that Herbert walked with giant steps so that I could hardly keep up with him. Then, suddenly he exclaimed, *"Goldene Freiheit!"* (golden freedom), revealing a confidence that surprised me. I looked up to his face and smiled at him.

6

Hiding in Berlin:
October 24, 1942–April 29, 1943

WE WERE ELATED! Here we were—both of us—walking side by side into the morning. The sun was shining on us: we were happy to be together and delighting in our escape. We realized that we had been unbelievably lucky to escape the Gestapo by seconds, not only once but twice. Two near-miracles had happened, almost too amazing to be believed. Yet they had happened! As we walked together, our thoughts still enveloped by these events, it became clear to me that I owed my life to Herbert. My strong attachment to him and the closeness we felt for each other had given me the impetus to run from the Gestapo. There was nothing else I could think of that would have made me dare an escape: the precipitous events of the night tied us together with a new bond that has grown and grown and become the defining moment in our lives.

After we had walked quietly for a while, Herbert broke the silence with an expletive: "Those bastards. Medieval conditions, removing you and your parents as witnesses of their crime. The principle of *Sippenhaft*!" (The term was used in feudal times and revived by the Nazis; it means the liability of all the members of a family for the deeds of one member.) I did not understand immediately what he meant, but Herbert explained it to me: "Your uncle in Switzerland, the owner of the house in which you lived in Kladow, has Argentine citizenship; therefore, he is a 'neutral alien' whose property rights have to be strictly observed. If they break this law, as they have done with the *Ritterkreuzträger*, and it becomes known, it can lead to bad publicity abroad or even to diplomatic démarches. That is why you and your parents had to disappear without fanfare, without even the usual preparedness for deportation. The whole family had to disappear, and the fewer people who know about it, the better.

You and your parents were eyewitnesses!" I understood. Previously, I had not seen our removal in that light, but the correlation became clear. They did not care to break international law. Who would know abroad—almost all foreign countries were in the enemy camp—that a law had been broken and who would care if a few more Jews were deported? Who could hold the Nazis to account?

Our momentary happiness was interrupted, and our thoughts recalled to reality. Both of us were determined to face the grim truth of our situation; both of us realized how difficult our lives in hiding might become. Could we trust our luck further? Could we find a few among the Germans to help us, knowing that (because of their help) they might endanger their own lives and the lives of their families? Could we even presume that they would? Well, to survive we at least had to try.

Our immediate problem was to find shelter for the first night of our underground life. I knew that I could turn to Putto, a close friend of many years who had previously offered her assistance should it become necessary. On this early Sunday morning, we made our way to her, to ask if her offer, given spontaneously at a visit in Kladow years before, still stood. We got a very friendly reception and accepted with gratitude the breakfast she served us. She listened with understanding to our story of the night's events and let us know how she empathized with us. Soon, though, we all were saddened, because she had to withdraw her earlier promise. She had approached her sleep-in maid without whose involvement the plan could not have succeeded, and asked her if she would be willing to tell a lie in order to save a life—a Jewish life—should that become necessary. The maid asked for time to think it over. After church, she gave Putto her answer: it was no. The young woman had spoken with her pastor about the problem, and the clergyman's reply was that it was more important to tell the truth than to save a life. It is difficult to believe that a pastor—of whatever church—could so coldheartedly make a decision against life and use such high-sounding moralistic principle in doing it. It struck me that Jews could not expect any sympathy, even in the most threatening circumstances, from the "Church of Christian Love and Salvation" ("die Kirche der christlichen Liebe und Erlösung"). On the contrary, I hold it as a truth that the church was fanning the hatred against the Jews into an antisemitic fervor that helped the Nazis to destroy the Jewish people.

The pastor's negative answer closed the possibility of our finding shelter with my friend. We all were painfully aware of that. Herbert and I would have to solve our problems, but Putto had to live with the burden of a broken promise. Later on, she felt that "fate was punishing her" for her failure with a life of unhappiness. On our frequent visits to her, which began in 1958 and have continued to the present, I have tried to dissuade her of this "crime and punishment" theory by telling her that: "I am your friend, and I survived and am living a happy life." Her answer comes promptly: "Yes, that is as it should be; you have deserved your happiness." Whenever and wherever we meet, her conversation returns to this point. I cannot stop her from repeatedly commenting on what she perceives as her "lifelong punishment." Her congratulations for my birthday arrive punc- tually and always say how happy she is that I am alive. I some- times hope, for her sake, that what she is telling me might be a slight exaggeration. Unfortunately, it does not seem so. For some people, their involvement in our fate had a devastating impact.

That Sunday morning at Putto's house our foremost thought was to find a place to sleep for the coming night. It was then that I remembered the envelope my mother had given me some time before with the remark that it contained some money and an address for an emergency. I had taken it furtively from Herbert's room seconds before leaving. I looked at it now, and seeing my mother's handwriting brought tears to my eyes: it was as if she had anticipated our desperate situation. I opened the envelope, and found the money, and a name, address, and telephone num- ber on a slip of paper. The name was unknown to me, and when we established the connection by phone, the answering voice gave me no clue: it was a strange voice, but became friendlier when I introduced myself as the daughter of Mrs. Schloss. When I asked if we could come to see them, the answer was affirma- tive. We would soon be on our way to Schmargendorf, a south- westerly borough of Berlin.

Before leaving Putto's, though, I needed to establish some connections for a variety of reasons. First, I had to let Christl

Simon know that we had gotten away the night before and that I hoped she could establish a "safe conduit to Switzerland" as soon as possible, as my aunt had hinted on her last visit to Berlin. We set up a date for me to visit her apartment the next day. The second phone call was to Aunt Ilse's mother, Mrs. Voigt, so that we might begin to establish a personal contact with my uncle and aunt in Switzerland as soon as feasible, and I might ask Mrs. Voigt a personal favor: to get for me some toiletries, a toothbrush and toothpaste, soap, comb and brush, and possibly a nightgown. She was willing to do that, and we agreed to meet the next afternoon not far from where she lived. The last phone call was to a co-worker—the only one I could reach—to arrange a meeting with him in the afternoon to ask him to take the message of our escape to Mr. Parlo and some of the people on my work team in the factory.

I also planned to pay two personal visits: one to my Uncle Ernst and Aunt Hedi to inform them of the happenings of the night before and of my parents' fate; the other, to Dr. Kassel's sister. I felt it prudent to warn Dr. Kassel not to return to the apartment in Niebuhrstrasse for fear that it was under Gestapo observation: it could become a real trap for her. Because I could not reach either one by telephone, I had to trust my luck to meet them at their homes.

We said our good-byes to Putto and set out for Schmargendorf. We found the address easily. We rang the bell, and when the door opened, I was surprised to look into two vaguely familiar faces. I had met this man and woman both recently in Kladow where they were visitors for an afternoon. I had not paid that much attention to them at the time, because Kladow usually attracted many visitors: our relatives and many of their friends, especially the large circle of Ernst and Hedi's bridge club, and friends and acquaintances I had made at the Emigration Department of the Reichsvereinigung. They all came to enjoy the privacy of the large garden, the view of the lake, and the freedom of being out of the city, to forget the constant threat to their lives for a few hours, and, last but not least, to enjoy my mother's hospitality. My mother was a wonderful baker: there was always an extra piece of cake she had prepared, and sometimes a gift from the garden to take home, depending on the season: some currant berries, some apples, a bouquet of flowers. How my mother had met the couple in Schmargendorf I do not know.

Without saying much, they motioned to us to enter the apartment and introduced themselves as "August" and "Else," as they said they wanted to be called. At first, this informality, not customary in Germany, seemed inappropriate to me, but we soon learned that they were secretive for a good reason. In underground situations, the threat of being caught always exists, and therefore the possibility that the name of your helpers would be tortured out of you.

Else and August were pleasant people in their fifties. They were very free with their own secrets: mother's introduction had made us confide in them, so they trusted us. We soon learned that the blonde Else was Jewish and lived in hiding with August, who was then and had always been, so he told us, a violent anti-Nazi. He had a Communist past, which he was hiding now. He showed us a portrait of Hitler that he had hanging on the wall: he turned it around, and on the reverse was a picture of Stalin. His attitude against the Nazis had gotten even stronger, because one of his sons had a high rank in the Nazi Party. In what he did, he wanted symbolically to prove his son wrong. It was quite clear that August was the dominant player in this situation; after all, he was Else's protector and was in the process of becoming ours. He had the zeal of a true believer, which manifested itself in the loud voice with which he advocated his beliefs. During our general conversation, he suddenly took me aside and asked me to tell him in detail the events of the previous night, especially what had happened to my parents. I told him, and at one point in my story he interrupted me, pronouncing in his stentorian voice: "You will never see your parents again!" The continuous flow of events during the past night and day and the necessity of facing reality had forced me to calm down, so that I had been able to maintain an outward calm. But this sudden and unexpected remark loosed a storm of emotions in me I could not hold back. The walls of my composure gave way, and I started crying like a child and could not stop. When August had left me, I was sitting on a chair by his desk; I lowered my head so that nobody should see my desperation. I knew with sudden clarity that he was right, that I could do nothing to help my parents escape the fate the Nazis had planned for them. My anger and sorrow completely overwhelmed me. I do not know why August made this remark to me in that situation. I have never forgotten that moment, which brought such terrible clarity!

Then, Herbert's voice called out for me, and when I rejoined the others, I heard the good news that August was willing to offer us a hiding place for the next few days. We were both relieved and grateful: it momentarily solved our greatest problem.

August was to show us the hiding place later in the afternoon, because I was anxious to be on my way to Dr. Kassel's sister's house to offer a warning in time for the coming night. I do not recall anymore where she lived or her married name. I only remember meeting a very serious woman who received my story with misgivings. Who could blame her for being upset that her sister's and possibly her own family's degree of danger had increased immeasurably? As we continued our conversation, she realized that the situation was not my fault and soon gave me the names of people who might be able to help us. Not long thereafter, Herbert made connections with them: Mr. Rieger, a white-haired trade-union man; Mr. Kottke, a hairdresser; the Weiner family in Weidmannshausen; and Ossi, a metal worker in the Borsig factory. All of them played a role in helping us to survive in our underground existence. Expressing my thanks and offering greetings to her sister, I left. I never saw her again. So many people met fleetingly on the Nazi stage of horror, to disappear from view forever. Where were they all going?

My next destination was the apartment of my uncle and aunt, who, after having been forced to give up their own apartment, were living with friends in Eisenzahnstrasse, at the corner of Kurfürstendamm. I wanted them to know what had happened to my parents and of my own and Herbert's escape. I had always felt very close to them, especially to my Aunt Hedi. Our meeting took a different turn from what I had expected: I had come to tell of my grief, but the friends with whom they shared the apartment, the Jakobsohns, were frightened to death by my story. Hedi was in tears but was unable to prevent their friends from threatening to inform on me unless I left immediately.

Ironically, the person they would have called to have me arrested was "Baby Mendelsohn," an official of the Jewish Congregation whom I had known since 1939 and whom I had introduced to Ernst and Hedi and to the Jakobsohn family as well. Mrs. Mendelsohn had been a frequent visitor in Kladow during less threatening times, but that had changed when she had became the Jewish coordinator for deportation transports leaving Berlin. It was obvious that I could not stop the Jakobsohns. By now, Hedi was dissolved in tears. I hugged her briefly and then was practically shooed out of the apartment with no good-byes from the others. I was upset and shaken by this scene and failed to understand how fellow Jews and especially my own family could reject me like that! I knew that they, like all Jews, felt threatened by deportation, but there was no danger to them at that particular moment. How could they of all people be the first to treat me like an outcast, the first to humiliate me, the first to prove that I had lost not only my dignity but my rights as well?

I knew that my aunt and uncle, too, were preparing their escape and were looking for a hiding place with the help of their former housekeeper, Mrs. Mielke. The Gedenkbuch lists Ernst and Hedi Bildesheim as deported to Auschwitz on June 28, 1943, "*Schicksal ungeklärt'* "—fate unknown.

As an afterthought to my description of the emotional and threatening scene in the Eisenzahnstrasse apartment, I feel compelled to give an explanation. More than fifty years have gone by since the events I am writing about. Why Jewish organizations were involved in the administration of the deportation of Jews to Eastern Europe still calls up acrimonious controversy. Unforgiving blame is heaped on such organizations, especially on German Jewish leadership.

At the time, we knew that only overwhelming power—and we Jews in Germany were the first to feel the "total threat"—could force our Jewish leaders to follow Nazi orders, as willful and arbitrary as those orders were. Not to fulfill the wishes of the Gestapo would mean more lawless conditions, more murders, more hostage shootings—in short, more "horror," though, in the end, the fate of the Jews could not have been more disastrous than it was.

Under pressure of force, the Jews were functioning as *Abhol-*

ers, aides at the collection points, at the train stations from where the transports to the East were leaving, or, at a higher level, as *Judenältester* in the ghettoes. The Jews who had to take on these functions were all the more endangered, because the Nazis would eliminate anybody who would not follow orders, or put to death those who had knowledge (or even an inkling) of their atrocities. That was true for people serving in the Berlin Reichsvereinigung, many of whom were deported in a transport in October 1942; the *Judenälteste* in Theresienstadt, Paul Eppstein; and the Jewish *Sonderkommandos* in the concentration camps, Jewish prisoners detailed to deal with the bodies of their exterminated fellow prisoners. "Baby Mendelsohn" also died in a concentration camp.

It was difficult to go on after this scene with my aunt and uncle, but my next meeting was prearranged by phone and could not easily be postponed. I was to meet the youngest of my co-workers—a fifteen-year old—at the Funktechnische Werkstätten where I had been forced to work. We had agreed to meet on a square right off the Kurfürstendamm, where he was waiting for me. In short outlines I told him what had happened the previous night, and asked him to tell some members of my work team confidentially, if he could—especially Mr. Parlo, the owner of the factory.

I had good reason to inform Mr. Parlo about my escape. He had foreseen that the day of disbanding the Jewish labor force would come and only a few months before, at the end of the summer, he had made an attempt to forewarn me.

When I first sought employment in his factory, in October 1941, Mr. Parlo interviewed me. Curiously, he had inquired about my reason for wanting to work in a factory. This question surprised me, because I had assumed that he might have known about the predicament of the Jews from the many Jewish workers in his employ. I explained that work in an armaments factory might protect me from deportation and, wanting him to understand that I was serious about working, explained that I lived far out in Kladow and would move to town to be on time for the morning shift if he hired me. He agreed immediately, and, it seemed to me, his attitude was very friendly. Our conversation had struck a personal note.

On his lapel Mr. Parlo wore the Nazi Party badge awarded for long-standing membership: the black swastika on a white background, surrounded by a broad golden rim. Many explanations for his wearing a swastika are possible, all of them conjectures. I knew that Mr. Parlo had intervened for some of his Jewish workers at the Nazi Labor Exchange, for example, hiring elderly Jewish workers. He had hired my mother to do "home work" for the factory and had also hired Mrs. Bielschowski, although she was in her seventies. Once, when I asked him to have a few days off to find out if emigration visas for such South American countries as Bolivia or Paraguay were obtainable, he warned me that these visas were nothing less than Gestapo traps. His understanding of our plight, if not clear until then although it should have been, was demonstrated one day in the late summer of 1942, when I had worked in the factory almost a year. He left a note at my workplace to appear in his office, which was across the street from the factory building, at a certain hour the next day. When I presented myself, he asked me to be seated across from him at his desk, then began into a commonplace conversation to which I reacted politely, but with reserve. I was nonplussed! Then, suddenly, he changed his approach and asked the following question: "What would you do if I could no longer protect my Jewish workforce from deportation?" He spoke with some vehemence, as if this sentence had been a major effort for him. He looked squarely at me, waiting for my answer. I was confused. Who could answer such a question at this time, with any certainty? Why had he asked me, just me? Suddenly I knew: he wanted a positive answer as a relief for himself. He wanted assurance from me that I would make an attempt to survive, because he had become acquainted with the defiant attitude I had shown.

Among the factory workers, conversations sometimes developed in which personal opinions were revealed. It did not happen often, but one particular time I was not careful to hide my feelings and was even defiant against the Nazi regime, as unwise or foolhardy as that was. As Mr. Parlo made his rounds with a young Jewish engineer and was possibly within hearing, a co-worker asked me what I would do after the war—possibly hint-ing at emigration. I responded that I would "come back to Berlin with the conquering Americans."

But such facetious daring was not suitable in answering the question Mr. Parlo asked me in his office. I took it for what it was: a most serious warning of what was to come. I felt helpless, not knowing what to think or what to say to him. With this question, he put me before an imaginary wall. How should I know now if I could climb it or not? It was an agonizing moment. Finally I said: "I will try to survive any way I can." It was probably the answer he had expected. His face did not show any visible relief, but with this question he had expressed his involvement. Then he said that he would let me know "when the time came." With that remark we parted.

"My time had come" earlier than he or I had anticipated, and I wanted him to know that I had escaped and would try to survive, as I had told him. Later, in May 1943, from Lausanne, Switzerland, I sent him a postcard with a view of Lake Geneva: it said "Greetings" and was signed Lotte Kladow.

During the next weeks in my underground time in Berlin I had no contacts with my former co-workers. Personal contact with them was too difficult to set up, and I had to avoid the neighborhood of the factory because the foreman and supervisor of the Jewish workers was an SA-man and a vicious antisemite. I never met anyone from the factory again. I also did not—and do not—know what happened to all of them on February 27, 1943. On that day, the SS conducted surprise raids on all factories where Jews were working. Without preparation all Jewish workers—7,000—were seized and sent to Auschwitz. It was the final destruction of the Berlin Jewish population. Did Mr. Parlo have any forewarnings of this "action"? If so, could he have given the workers a sign that might have forestalled the worst? I am sure that he would have done what he could to save them, but was it in his power to do so?

When Herbert and I returned to Berlin the first time after the war, in 1958, we could not find Mr. Parlo. All traces led nowhere, so any thanks due him could never be said. My gratitude to him remains undiminished.

All my errands accomplished, I felt that I had done for the day what I had set out to do. The day, the first day after our escape, was almost over, and it would soon be time to look at our hiding place. I yearned for it and returned to Schmargendorf, where August and Else—and Herbert, of course—were waiting for me.

When it was dark, August took us to our hiding place. He was a house painter and had rented a basement, where he had stored his painting equipment. Adjacent to the storage area was a small alcove furnished with two couches, with a small table in between; some makeshift bookshelves served as walls. It had a cellar window toward the street, hung with heavy draperies so that no ray of candlelight could penetrate to the outside. The blackout had to be strictly observed, especially in our case. The only bathroom sink and toilet were across the cellar, past a heap of coal, and, no matter how easily we tread, a wooden board would always make noise. The cellar was an open space, and the possibility existed that the superintendent of the building, attending the boiler, might surprise us. We could come only in the evening and had to leave early in the morning. The security of this space was questionable, and it became clear that we must look for a safer hiding place soon. August also explained to us that there was to be no contact between him and Else and us. We were on our own from now on. We never saw August and Else again, other than to return the key of the cellar when we left and to tell them how relieved and grateful we were for the first night's shelter, which they had granted us.

For many years after the war, the Holocaust got the silent treatment in Germany, as if, if it were not talked about, the Holocaust would fade into the past. This long silence was broken when the younger generation began to ask questions. This process took place over many years, as more Germans joined in and the German government set up new institutions dealing with the Nazi period, the fate of the survivors and their helpers. Some of the former concentration camps, like Dachau and Bergen-Belsen, were made into memorials and their staff did research on the documents of former inmates. The knowledge about the Holocaust is a painfully slow developing story, whose details are still emerging.

A recent letter (1999) from Berlin informed us about the fate of August and Else: after more than half a century, we learned their full names for the first time—August Sapandowski and Elsbeth Orgler.

Only a few weeks after Herbert and I had left the cellar, the people then hiding there were denounced: they were arrested and the cellar sealed. August and Else went into hiding for several months in southern Germany, but were arrested in May 1943 after their return to their apartment in Berlin. Else's name disappears from the record for a short period, but turns up a few months later on August 4, 1943, on a list, together with ninety-nine other names on the "40th Osttransport" from Berlin to Auschwitz, where she probably was killed upon arrival.

August was interrogated and held in prison for three months, then released. Soon thereafter, however, he was rearrested when he was denounced for hiding Jews in his apartment. This time, he was transferred to Sachsenhausen and Bergen-Belsen concentration camps, where he died after three months. The death certificate signed by the Waffen SS doctor states that he died of a "circulatory disorder" and gives the date of his death as March 11, 1945, about one month before Bergen-Belsen was liberated by British troops.

Among August's possessions was a poem of his. I include two lines from it: "Bange machen gilt hier nicht / Kämpfe recht heisst Deine Pflicht" (Don't be frightened / Fight for what you think is right). It was August's credo and a fitting epitaph to his life.

I do not remember exactly how I survived this first day of our escape with all its anxieties and activities, meetings with people, and their reactions. I do not remember whether I ate or not. It did not matter to me any longer not to have clean underwear tomorrow, nor did it bother me to know how we could buy food the next day without ration cards. The day came to an end and with it my energy; I fell asleep.

The next morning, we left the shelter very early. Somehow, we had breakfast and lunch, but I do not remember where the necessary food stamps came from. And then we did something unexpected. We went to the zoo, the first visit of many to follow. Whenever Herbert and I had time on our hands, we went to the zoo at the Joachimsthaler Strasse, in the center of West Berlin. It was a famous zoo with many buildings in a large park. Later on, when we had separate hiding places and came from different directions to meet in town, we frequently met at the zoo at the elephant house. It was our usual rendezvous. As long as the weather held, we just had to mix with a group of tourists looking at or feeding the elephants. When the weather was inclement, and it had become colder, we added visits to the aquarium. Being at the zoo made us feel safe, as safe as wearing a magic hat. We did not believe that the Gestapo would look for Jews in a zoo. The zoo was also a safe place to talk, which became important to us when we were planning our escape to Switzerland.

In the afternoon of this second day, I had two appointments. The first meeting was with Christl Simon. I went to her apartment at the Fehrbelliner Platz. It was furnished with elegance in a sportive English style, decorated with many engravings of horses and English hunting scenes, which, I thought, fitted Christl Simon to a T. She impressed me as a straightforward person, determined, and somewhat masculine. Her behavior toward me was direct, friendly, and open. She introduced me to her Jewish doctor friend whom she was hiding in her apartment. (After the war Christl was awarded a medal for having saved Jewish lives: her name is inscribed on a tablet of honor in Yad Vashem in Jerusalem.) On her last visit in Berlin, my Aunt Ilse had spoken to Christl about a "conduit" to Switzerland and the way to reach my aunt and uncle in an emergency. Ilse had also hinted to me about this connection and added that I would get the name of this "mystery person" from Christl, in case of an emergency. Christl was ready to give me the name but not before I had promised to keep it secret so as not to endanger this person and the organization whose employee he was. I promised, of course. His name was Jean Friedrich, a Swiss; his organization, the International Red Cross. I had to learn his address and telephone number by heart. Two days later I was to meet him at the Ballenstedter Strasse 2, where the Red Cross used a villa for office space and representation. I left Christl with greater confidence than I had come with.

Next I was to meet Mrs. Voigt, Ilse's mother. I was waiting for her in the street, not far from her apartment. When she approached me, I saw how frail a woman she was and how pale she looked. Her eyes expressed sadness, and I felt her sympathy for the fate of my parents without her expressly saying anything. When she handed me the little parcel of toiletries I had asked her to buy for me, she gave me a message from Henriette Schneider. I was to go to the office of my uncle's real estate company, Firma Schürmann & Schmidt, at the corner of Unter den Linden and Friedrich Strasse the next afternoon. I did not know what to make of this message. I had no idea what they might want from me: in its urgency it had an almost ominous ring.

The next afternoon, when I walked into the Schürmann & Schmidt offices, my anxiety was confirmed. I was ushered into their conference room and seated at a round table where three people were waiting for me, Mr. Schürmann, Mr. Schmidt, and Miss Henriette Schneider, all of whom were known to me; the two men I knew vaguely, but Miss Schneider had been a long-time acquaintance of our family, even a friend of my mother's. I had great respect for her, mixed, however, with some irreverence. She was the successor to my uncle's business, Spitzenhaus M. Schöneberg, which had been transferred to her pro forma, to steer it through Nazi times as an "Ayran" firm, which she did. Ludwig had handed the reins of Firma Schöneberg to her because he fully trusted her. The amusing aspect of her person was that she could have been a nineteenth-century fashionplate in a Prussian vignette: she wore long skirts and full blouses, always in black, with an inset of netting held up by stays ending under her chin. Her hair was piled up high on her head, held there by pins and a large clasp in the back. She was definitely an imposing personality. She favored a clipped style of speaking, which reinforced the impression of rigidity and self-importance. She was the perfect caricature of Potsdam virtue and tradition.

Miss Schneider opened the conversation. During the hour that followed, she was the dominant speaker. The two men kept rather quiet and mostly nodded their agreement with what she said, with an air of benevolence. The more she talked, the more frightened I became. It was obvious that I had been thrust into the role of villain. Mrs. Voigt had informed Miss Schneider that Herbert and I had run from the Gestapo. Miss Schneider said, "Though you have escaped the Gestapo, there is no way out for you." She suggested to me that the only solution for me was to give myself up to the Gestapo and join my parents on the transport to the East! I was stunned by what she said: I could not understand or believe what I had heard. Had a friend really said that? I was silent: I could not trust my voice. She continued: "You must do that now, immediately, before the transport of your parents leaves the Levetzowstrasse!" I asked myself if she believed that I could be of assistance to my parents on their way to a *Konzentrationslager* or help them during their stay there? But before I could ask her, she explained her reasons for her suggestion: "Germany is winning this war and, before it is over, Germany will have conquered Europe and Russia: Germany will rule all of Europe and Russia. You will look in vain for a hiding place in any of these conquered countries. Giving up now is the best solution!" She continued, "You are dark and Jewish-looking. There will be no chance for you!" I was so shaken by such brutality coming from someone I believed was a family friend. Still, in a low voice I made clear to them that I would not do what they had suggested, then rose and left.

On my visits to Berlin in 1958 and 1963, I met Henriette Schneider again: neither of us ever mentioned this scene.

While I was going through these experiences, Herbert, too, was very busy meeting people and searching out possibilities for a new hiding place. Though we were happy being together, we both knew it was not safe in the long run. One morning, as I crossed the open space in the cellar, I had seen the silhouette of the superintendent as he was leaving the basement, and I was not sure whether he had seen me too. It became urgent for us to find a new place. Herbert met Mr. Rieger, Mrs. Kassel's trade-union man and had come away with the impression that he would try to find a new domicile for us. But everything needed time. I had taken up with some of my old contacts in Kladow who might be helpful for Herbert: our old family doctor in Kladow, who had married into a Christian family; and Mr. Strindberg, a friend of his and the son of August Strindberg, who was working at the time in Berlin, as a journalist at the *Berliner Illustrirte Zeitung*, a weekly that resembled *Life* Magazine. Both expressed their willingness to give Herbert temporary shelter, but that had to be postponed until I found a new hiding place too.

On one of the days shortly after our escape, we visited the Mecklenburgische Allee, the place my parents had lived for only a few weeks, the place where I had said good-bye to them so recently, the place I hated to remember. Still, I felt an obligation to visit it once more, to see if they had left anything to remember them by. But there was nothing left to take with me. After the war, we returned once more to "that place." We could not find it. The houses had been bombed out, and the street name was now Marathon-Allee.

We tried to reestablish as many contacts as we could, because new ones needed time to develop. We could find some of our old friends by looking up their names in the telephone book. It was in that simple way that we found Wanda Dombrowski again. She and her husband—theirs was a mixed, Christian–Jewish marriage—were old friends of Uncle Ludwig's going back to before World War I. When Leo Dombrowski emigrated to Brazil in 1937, Wanda had promised to join him, but she had delayed it for some reason. By now, it seemed that her stay in Berlin had become permanent. She was a cheerful woman in her fifties; her laughter was contagious. She made a living as a corsetière, making girdles and corsets for private customers. The sewing machine was usually going when we came, but she would gladly interrupt her work to have a chat with us and to share whatever she had. We spent many hours in her apartment—a little oasis, though cramped in space. Her trade allowed her to give me some underwear I was very much in need of, and, later on, she and her skill with the snap-fastener machine were instrumental in attaching a photo on Herbert's identification papers.

It was not until one of our visits in the late 1970s that we found her new address in Berlin—she had been totally bombed out. We visited her and found her as cheerful as ever but not in good health. We left her saddened. But she accepted life as it was.

Another companion was Lutz (Ernst Ludwig) Ehrlich, a former fellow student of Herbert's at the Hochschule für die Wissenschaft des Judentums (Lehranstalt). He, his mother, and their housekeeper, Emma, lived in the Windscheidt Strasse. He felt very close to Herbert. One day Lutz told us that his mother had gotten the order for deportation, and he was desperate to convince her to feign suicide. Could we help to convince her? The scheme he was thinking of was to give her six tablets of Veronal just before the Gestapo came to pick her up; the Veronal would put her into a deep sleep, but it certainly would not be a fatal dose. When she fell asleep, Emma would immediately call the Jewish Hospital in the Iranischen Strasse and tell them that Mrs. Ehrlich had committed suicide. The ambulance would come, take her to the hospital, her stomach would be pumped out, and she would be as good as before. The delay of the deportation date might then allow her enough time to go into hiding. It seemed likely that the plan would succeed and we agreed, if Mrs. Ehrlich accepted it, to help in snatching a victim out of the Gestapo's clutches.

Mrs. Ehrlich was willing to risk it, so one day we assembled in a bedroom in the Windscheidt Strasse. Mrs. Ehrlich was in bed and ready to swallow the six tablets. There was a right way and a wrong way to take them. There had to be an interval between swallowing each one and a liquid to drink to make the body accept them. It would therefore take a certain time for her to fall asleep. She was very anxious; so were we all. I sat on her bed, took her hand in mine, and asked her to tell me how she felt after taking a tablet. At first, she told me that she was quite comfortable; she had no adverse stomach reaction. A few minutes later she reported seeing undefined landscapes and color globs before her eyes; she began to mumble. We watched her falling asleep. and Emma was on the phone calling the hospital. We left before the ambulance came. I felt depressed: had I assisted in beating death? Was there no end of this wrangle with death?

Almost everything happened as Lutz had predicted: they pumped her stomach out, and she slowly recovered. However, she told me that she never regained her old strength, and it turned out that the plan was carried out in vain: Mrs. Ehrlich did not make up her mind quickly enough to go into hiding. Instead she returned to her factory work and was apprehended with all the other Jewish workers, on February 27, 1943, and deported. She was one of the 7,000 shipped directly to Auschwitz.

Her son Lutz had gone underground before this point, the only person I knew who had chosen it on his own initiative. I did not know where he was hiding. We met at regular intervals, and I introduced him to Wanda. The Ehrlichs transferred all their possessions to Emma for safekeeping, so the money that Lutz needed had to come from her. Because he could not show up in his old home, it was natural that I became his messenger. I don't know how many endearing words come up in my mind to describe Emma: she dutifully served her family; she was devoted and true to her principles—in short, she was a wonderful person. She had a round face and only her blue eyes were remarkable about her face; her figure was stout, in part because she wore black peasant garb, nineteenth-century style. When I approached her with Lutz's requests for money, she was always very willing to give it to me but excused herself for a moment and turned slightly away to lift her skirt and then her underskirts—all of them black—until she had found the one, the right one, with the sewn-in pocket, from which she took the money and handed it to me. It was always an expected and slightly funny moment for me. I kept a serious face so as not to offend her dignity. I always thanked her in Lutz's name and left. She saved the Ehrlichs' possessions throughout the war and later gave them back to Lutz. He told us that she became very old, kept all her capacities, and was well cared for in her old age.

A few days after my disastrous encounter with Miss Schneider, I went to meet Mr. Jean Friedrich, the Red Cross representative. As I walked toward the Ballenstedter Strasse, my thoughts went back to that ugly scene with the moneychangers. It had left so many confusing impressions that I tried to clear up in my mind. I was almost sure that at the time, the end of October 1942, many Germans were of the same opinion as Miss Schneider: Germany would win the war. How often were we depressed when advances and victories were announced with fanfare over the radio! How often did we wish for an early end that would spare Jewish lives!

We were cut off from contacts with the outside world, read, and heard nothing but the din of victories, yet we knew of the other world of the "great powers," the Allies fighting Germany, and we asked ourselves: "Could they really lose?" In Germany, the Nazi government and its followers were intoxicated with their successes and expected the *Endsieg*, the final victory—as predicted by Miss Schneider's brash assurances—to be theirs.

Could it possibly be true? At such moments, it felt as if we were hoping against hope.

I had left the meeting with Miss Schneider with deep resentment. It had awakened fears in me I was trying to still, as I worried about the difficulties that lay ahead. Now Miss Schneider had thrown into doubt our belief that survival made sense. She exuded Nazi propaganda and national "optimism," of course, but how many Germans thought as she did? Would I not find people to help me because I "looked Jewish"? Would they also believe that I had no chance to survive? I felt apprehension rising in me, even as I told myself she had to be wrong. What if nobody would help because it would be so hopeless? Did I have to feel guilty because I thought I could escape from the belly of the monster? Miss Schneider had planted deep distrust in me that I could not overcome easily, maybe not at all. It was the cause of new conflicts that arose and stayed with me.

My apprehension dropped away as soon as Mr. Friedrich greeted me. His welcome was cordial. It became clear to me that he had come from another world. His good manners and his interest were palpable; with his Swiss urbanity and politesse, he had something of the diplomat about him. He understood what yesterday's accountants had harshly denied: my need to be encouraged and reassured. It helped that he was also a good-looking, even dashing young man.

It seemed as if he had all the time in the world as he sat opposite me and listened to the story of our escape and the deportation of my parents. I felt that only he could understand the extent of the terror that had struck my family. I stressed the urgency of informing my uncle of these events: his knowing would relieve me immeasurably. There was no question that Mr. Friedrich listened with sympathy, and he told me that he would gladly do what I wished him to do. I assumed that he would inform my uncle and felt easier. All my life my uncle had been the head of our family; he needed to know what had happened to my parents. I also hoped that I could depend on his help and his resources to assist us in this emergency.

Expressing my gratitude to Mr. Friedrich, I concluded that our conversation had come to an end, but I was wrong. Mr. Friedrich started to ask some questions on his own: he wanted to know

documents and the correspondence of that time, were later given to us: the only document missing was my four-page letter. Our guess is that he very likely used it as proof to the Swiss authorities of how endangered my life in Germany was in an attempt to convince the Swiss to open their border to Jews who were fleeing for their lives. At the time, the Swiss motto for withstanding the pressure for more immigration was "The Boat Is Full!" Many Jews who attempted to enter Switzerland at the time, when Southern France was occupied by the Nazis, were sent back, sometimes right into the arms of the Gestapo. With the beginning of 1943, however, there was a change in policy after a concerted campaign had begun and rumors of the extermination policy decided at the Wannsee Conference in January 1942 had reached the Swiss public. (This policy, executed by the SS under Adolf Eichmann and Reinhard Heydrich, had been officially sanctioned at a secret conclave of high German civil servants and SS leaders held in Berlin on January 20, 1942, the notorious Wannsee Conference.)

When Mr. Friedrich next talked to me, he acquainted me with the plan of an escape to Switzerland. I was surprised at his suggestion, and my first reaction was negative. My concern was Herbert. The belief that my initial escape from the Gestapo had precipitated Herbert into underground existence was very much alive in me. For that reason—leaving out of consideration my love for him and his for me—I could not fathom leaving him alone in that situation, which I had created, though involuntarily. It simply did not enter my head that I would seek safety just for myself. As I saw it, one of us could not survive without the other, what happened to one happened to the other, what we were experiencing brought us together, nothing should tear us apart. I do not recollect if I told Mr. Friedrich of these thoughts in so many words, but I demanded that, if an escape was to be planned, it had to include both of us. Mr. Friedrich understood that I would insist on this condition.

Mr. Friedrich was ready with advice and encouragement. He presented his view of the basic aspect of the current and developing conditions for Jews living in hiding. It was his opinion that with every day our lives would become more endangered. The tense war situation would make underground life increas-

ingly difficult for us. He had come to the conclusion that the
storm unleashed against the Jews would take on whirlwind pro-
portions. From 1939 on, Hitler had been threatening the Jews
with annihilation if a new world war would break out. It was
clearly absurd and illogical, as if the war he had started was
caused by "world Jewry." Revenge and spite dominated Nazi
thinking, and Hitler had the power to act on this absurdity. I
did not doubt Mr. Friedrich's assessment of the situation. As an
individual, as a diplomat, and now as a Red Cross official dealing with prisoner of war camps, he knew what he was talking
about. I trusted his experiences and observations, and I trusted
him as a human being. I knew that he wanted to save our lives.
I accepted his plan of escape for both of us. When I attempted
to express my gratitude to him, he wanted none of it: he did
what he did as an involvement that came natural to him. Before
I left, he mentioned that he would be going on home leave for a
short time and that he would meet my uncle and impress on
him the necessity of finding a way for us to escape to Switzerland soon. I noted the urgency with which he was following the
plan of our escape.

The next time I went to see Mr. Friedrich he gave me an envelope with money he said had come indirectly from my uncle to
assist us. He, Mr. Friedrich, was the intermediary and would act
as such in the future. I was astounded by how much money it
was and told him so, but he insisted that it was necessary "to
pay our way" and listed quite a few uses for the money, such as
finding and paying for a new hiding place, buying food and
ration cards on the black market, and, taking the long view, the
possible need for false identification papers. During the last two
weeks we had spent most of the money Herbert had and what
my mother had left in the envelope marked for "emergencies."
So far, it had been enough, but I recognized that Mr. Friedrich,
in his estimation of our situation, might have the clearer insight
of what we needed, so I accepted the money with gratitude.

It was not an easy decision for us to leave our hiding place in
August's cellar: it had not offered much physical comfort, but
we had been together and that was what counted most when we
weighed the pros and cons of our frightening situation. But this
balance was upset because we no longer felt safe. Building su-

perintendents were often informants for the Nazis. They had a list of the residents and were to report to the police if they saw some new and unregistered person entering the building regularly. They were admonished to be suspicious. If they were also paid for their spying services, I cannot say. It would also have been naïve of us not to take this situation fully into account. Our decision was to leave.

The white-haired trade-union man had found a shelter for me: it was to be in Weidmannshausen, all the way in the north of Berlin, where a family named Weiner owned a grocery store: a mom-and-pop store. They were willing to give me temporary shelter—temporary because the accommodations they had for themselves were very small, and it was really a sacrifice for them to share them with me. A further disadvantage was that the house stood by itself and anybody entering it could be seen clearly. Alhough shoppers did come and go, in a small community like that, a stranger might be looked at with curiosity. A spider web of suspicion was being woven over all of Germany. I could not leave the house very often, and when I did I had to return after dark.

The Weiners were nice and gentle people, and they liked having me with them. Unlike August, they were quietly assured of their Communism and did not endanger themselves by provocative behavior. The little room behind the store was my day room, but I could not move much or make any sound because the swing-door to the store had a small glass window. Because my presence had to be kept a secret from any customer, it followed that I had to be as quiet as a mouse. It was a vexing situation for me, but the only way to be secure for the moment. Herbert had found accommodations with Mr. and Mrs. Strindberg in Kladow, so we could not see each other often but were in touch by phone.

All day we looked forward to the evening, when the BBC (British Broadcasting Company) would send evening news. We huddled around the radio to catch every word from the beginning when the well-known voice of the announcer said: "This is the BBC, this is London speaking" and we heard the bells of Big Ben strike the hour. We listened with rapt attention.

A few events during the war revived our hope: the first of

these was the attack on Russia on June 21, 1941. Herbert and I remembered that Sunday afternoon when we had met at Pichelsdorf, at the corner of Heerstrasse, and listened in silence, during a tram ride, to the German war hubris: "In five weeks we will be in Moscow!"

The winter that year, 1941–42, was so cold that the whole Wannsee froze over, which did not happen very often. I remember seeing some German soldiers with heavily bandaged feet being carried on stretchers to waiting ambulances from a special train at the Bahnhof Charlottenburg, where Willi Mayer and I took off for work to the factory when it was still dark in the early morning hours during the winter months.

The second step up in our hope occurred in December 1941 when, after the attack by the Japanese on Pearl Harbor on December 7, 1941, Hitler declared war on the United States. But neither of these events were able yet to reverse German successes. Though it gave us pause to think that they had not conquered Moscow "in five weeks" and had also not taken Leningrad, German attacks by submarines on Allied convoys had continued and Allied losses were heavy. German successes were described as "huge successes" in the *Völkische Beobachter*, "weakening the Allied war effort altogether."

But now, in the middle of November 1942, the BBC announcer's voice was not quite so sedate as it had been before, and as we listened, we became more and more excited about the news we heard. The Allies had landed in North Africa and had established a bridgehead that was steadily enlarging. The first reports of an encirclement move around the entire Sixth Army before Stalingrad came in December. These two events appeared to be of tremendous importance as turning points in the war. They helped to ease the anxiety I carried away from the meeting with Miss Schneider, and Mr. Friedrich's confidence seemed more and more confirmed.

As the BBC broadcasts continued during the month of November, we learned that the Allied army under Field Marshall Montgomery had defeated the German and Italian armies under Field Marshall Rommel in the Battle of El Alamein in North Africa, and the day-by-day reports from Stalingrad told us about the complete encirclement of 250,000 German soldiers at Stalingrad, their ordeal, and their surrender to the Russians. German radio fanfares rejoiced in the unbelievable bravery of the German troops and their endurance in the weeks of encirclement. Losses were rarely mentioned. Death notices published by the afflicted families spoke of *stolze Trauer*, pride in mourning their losses.

The fortunes of war had turned against the Germans for the first time. We were buoyed by these events, but they had no immediate influence on our lives: quite the contrary. As Mr. Friedrich had predicted, the Nazis doubled their effort to destroy us. There was no turning around for them, neither in their policy toward us nor in any decision to end the war. Did they already know then that nobody would accept or believe their will to peace?

After I had been at the Weiners' for a week or two, a visit was arranged with one of their political friends who had a small cottage in one of the garden colonies that dotted the environs of Berlin. Herbert was invited too. We met one Sunday afternoon for coffee and cake at hairdresser Kottke's cottage. He and his wife belonged to the same Communist circle. He was a tall man, dark-haired, and rather effusive. While we were talking freely about the political situation, he suddenly mentioned that he had hidden a few rifles under his porch: the "time may come when we need them." I did not understand precisely which "time" he was alluding to, but I thought him absolutely crazy to fight with a gun in his hands against a giant juggernaut. Still, his comments showed that the idea of "resistance by the oppressed" in such a monster state was still alive. But what would he and we gain? Not only would he lose his life but others would lose theirs as well; there would be many victims of such heroic action. Of course, Mr. Kottke never mentioned that Communist plans for such an uprising would be set in motion only as the Red Army was arriving, and the locals would act as guerrillas to support it. He would set in motion a deadly game of retaliation and hostage-killing—a game at which the Nazis were masters. Wasn't he aware that when a few young Jewish Communists set fire to an anti-Communist exhibition—a blaze that had not caused much damage—not only had the perpetrators been killed but the whole young Communist group of sixteen were beheaded?

All the members of the Baum-Gruppe are buried in the cemetery of Weissensee. They are heroes now! They died in vain.

When SS Führer Heydrich was assassinated in Czechoslovakia, all the men in the village of Lidice were shot, the women sent to a concentration camp—Ravensbrück—the village burned and leveled. And the Jews, always the immediate victims, were not exempt from this massacre. Reichsminister Goebbels had 250 Jews arrested in Berlin: of these 50 were shot immediately, and the others sent to a concentration camp. The events in Lidice were publicized in horrid detail as mean revenge more than cold deterrence. How much success would Mr. Kottke have? How many victims would his resistance cost? From the beginning, the Nazis had labeled the Communists enemy no. 1: during the Weimar Republic, they had fought them in street battles and later invented the Reichstag fire and punished the Communists for it. In 1941, they had attacked Russia to eradicate "Communism root and branch." In the conquered Eastern countries the SS had orders to execute all Communist leaders first.

When the Nazis would start another wave of arrest against Communists, especially in Berlin, even without provocation, was anyone's guess: it could well be next week or next month. Herbert and I felt that Mr. Kottke, who spoke in such zealous tones about his plans, would add a new degree of danger to my life, that I might become involved in it as a guest of the Weiner family. We wanted to survive. As kindly as Mom and Pop Weiner were treating me, it became necessary to find a different shelter.

After the war, when we returned for a visit to Berlin from the United States, I could not locate either the Kottke or the Weiner families.

By good luck a new shelter was found for me. Within a short time I was installed in an apartment in the Bregenzer Strasse 14, in West Berlin, near the Olivaer Platz. It was a large and airy apartment that belonged to General Marcks of World War I fame. At the time I moved in, he had been a recluse for some years: he wanted to be undisturbed by the world in order to write his memoirs. He employed an elderly housekeeper, Alma, who served him meals in his room, which he rarely left. It was through Hella Gorn that I joined the Marcks household.

It was entirely accidental that Herbert, in trying to extend our circle of contacts, had met the Heilmanns, a Jewish family well-known in public and political circles at the time because Mr. Heilmann had been the Faction Chief of the Social Democratic Party in the Prussian parliament during the Weimar period and an outstanding foe of the Nazis. He was one of the first victims after the Nazi *Machtübernahme*—after the Nazis' seizure of power in 1933. They interned him in the concentration camp Oranienburg, where he was kept for six years. I was told by his son Peter that he was severely mistreated and then tortured to death in 1938–39.

Herbert first met Mr. Heilmann's sister-in-law and then was introduced by her to his son Peter and to Peter's girlfriend, Hella Gorn. She worked as a secretary, but had also taken on the task of informing General Marcks, for one hour daily, of important events taking place on the outside, because he refused to read newspapers. This obligation formed the basis of her stay in his apartment. When Peter and Hella heard of our story, Hella was ready to take me in. That she belonged to a group of young German Quakers accounts for her willingness to help. It was surprising that there was an empty room in the apartment. I later heard from Alma, the housekeeper, that the previous in-habitant had been deported in 1941 with the transport to the East of "stateless Jews"; nobody else said anything about this. I was glad to have a room of my own and the use of a regular bathroom.

I was introduced to General Marcks in a formal manner and to Alma and the woman-superintendent in a less formal way. The story Hella invented was that I had come from Munich, where air raids had destroyed several buildings in Schwabing, the area where I had supposedly lived. My appearance and the lack of clothing and papers were thus accounted for—at least, for the Marcks household, some neighbors, and the superinten-dent. Of course, I could not tell this invented story to the police.

It soon turned out that Hella was a domineering and willful person. She had developed a strong prejudice against Herbert and forbade him to visit at Bregenzer Strasse. She also made an attempt to separate us, because she believed that our attachment would only bring grief to me: it would be much better for me to form a new friendship with one of the young men in the group of "Friends"—the Quakers. I was stunned. When I asked her why, she told me in aggrieved accents that Herbert resembled her first boyfriend, who had been a "bad person," and repeated that she "did not wish to have any contact with him."

I thought her reasoning so twisted that it could merely be a pretext to hide her true feelings. But what were they? I never found out. On one side of her personality was a willingness to help; on the other, sudden aggressiveness. What she gave with one hand, she took with the other. Her behavior gave me many tense moments during our long relationship, which, as it progressed, became more unbalanced. At the end of my stay, shortly before the planned escape, I became really frightened of what she might do. I could not forget for one moment that I was dependent on her. I rued this dependency. However much one owes in gratitude to such a person is diminished by the unjust exercise of his or her power. It makes one doubly aware of the loss of freedom.

During this difficult period, aggravated by Hella's bizarre behavior, I had considerable personal support from a friend of my former husband's whose great human strength was in strange contrast with the dilemma of loyalty and politics he was trying to work out in his life.

Klix came from an old military family. His father was a brigadier general or something akin. I cannot recognize military ranks properly. Klix had grown up in a conservative atmosphere, and it might have been the reason for his joining the Nazi Party in 1931–32. He always stressed to me that he had become disillusioned with the Party very quickly, but did not officially resign from it, when resignation did not yet have a political price attached to it, as was the case once the Nazis were in power. He was a radical conservative nationalist. The Nazis' foreign policies he saw as basically identical to the policies the old German conservative elites had pursued and the Weimar Republic had deserted. The Nazis would return Germany to its imperial glory. He was, of course, aware of the considerable crudeness of the Nazi style of politics, and he strongly despised the antisemitism of their thought and behavior. Nobody could have overlooked this antisemitism, because Hitler had turned it from "a mere religious prejudice," which was tolerated in Germany until then, into an all encompassing national race hatred. Klix considered himself a philo-Semite and showed this attitude as often as he could.

He had expressed his sympathy with me when I divorced my husband, Wolfram, a German man. He had invited me to a party in his parents' home while I was working in the armaments factory. When I did not want to accept the invitation, he made it a personal point of honor. I gave in. His father and mother must have known who I was and treated me with special friendliness.

I recall that I felt unhappy at this party. I believed that I was there under false pretenses, and I wished not to be identified in anybody's thinking with conservative political aims. I rejected these people's moral indifference and their treatment of minorities, which included my own people as well as the oppressed in the countries they conquered. They had supported a political cause for which millions had to die. They had gone to war for Hitler. I realized that under no conditions should I be attending this party and left as early as I could.

How much Klix shared in the Nazis' foreign policy delusions was made apparent to me on the day, June 21, 1941, when the Nazis invaded Russia. I remember the scene with him as if it were today: we were walking along the Leibnizstrasse, where he lived, when he told me cheerfully, "In five weeks we will be in Moscow!" I looked at him in open disbelief and said, "I don't believe you!" Having learned well my history lesson of Napoleon's lost war in Russia, I continued, "In my opinion the war in Russia will add to the German war difficulties." Klix, having his own superior war logistics, did not take my answer very seriously. His illusions proved that his identification with the Nazi war aims seemed to be complete. The truth dawned on me that I should no longer have anything to do with him. But I could not bring myself to say this to him.

During the war, his military background, his conservative thinking, his education, and early membership in the Party led to a speedy rise in the hierarchy and an important position in the intelligence service. If events after 1941—the planned destruction of the Jews in the East, the "massacre of the political commissars" on Hitler's orders, the disintegration of the Ger-

man *Wehrmacht*, all of which Klix witnessed with his own eyes—
had wrought any change in his thinking, I cannot say.

During the winter of 1942–43, Klix was severely wounded by
shrapnel on the Russian front. In January or February 1943 he
asked Herbert and me to visit him in the Lazarett Hospital in
Berlin-Tempelhof. It was on this occasion that he spoke of offering Herbert his identification papers. A few weeks later, when
Klix was on crutches, Herbert and he had lunch together in one
of the restaurants on the Kurfürstendamm, and this time Klix
offered his papers in earnest: they indicated that Klix was an
officer of the SD, a branch of the SS intelligence service. Herbert
and I had to recognize his mad courage. If Herbert were caught
with this kind of identification papers, both of them—Herbert as
well as Klix—would have lost their heads. On Klix's part it was
no less than high treason. Herbert thanked Klix, but "respect-
fully declined" to accept these papers because of the danger.

After the war, we heard that Klix had given shelter to a Jewish
woman who survived the war because of this action. When we
met him in Berlin after the war, he mentioned to us that he had
done a service for us of which we were yet unaware: on June 13,
1943, the day on which Herbert was to cross the border, Klix had
received a telephone call from Hella Gorn, my former underground hostess, asking him to have Herbert arrested by the Gestapo, when he would cross the Swiss border, and giving the
particulars of place and time. Klix, of course, did not inform the
Gestapo about Herbert but did not tell Hella Gorn that he had
not done so, for fear that she might do so herself.

The end of the war left bitterness in Klix because, although he
had helped us and others, for which he had letters of corrobora-
tion, he had failed to mention to the "De-Nazification authorities" his early Nazi Party membership and was therefore
sentenced to prison for perjury. He always felt that an injustice
had been done to him. During the years after the war, he served
frequently in German courts as an authority on Nazi uniforms
and insignia. He was the expert on these less important matters;
never was he called as a witness in a Nazi war crimes trial.

As a member of the Marcks household, my life became more
orderly and comfortable, too, compared with what it had been
in August's cellar, near a heap of coals, or in the Weiners' room

behind the store. It was probably just this well-ordered life where everybody was well dressed that made me feel like the poor relation in comparison. I was so tired of having only one dress, one light coat, and one pair of shoes with just one change of underwear. It was a matter of cleanliness, too. It was wintertime now, and the Nazis were again collecting warm clothes for *Winterhilfe* (winter aid), indicating how much they needed them. Without a ration card for textiles, which I could not get, I could not buy anything new. I needed some of my former belongings. Why not get my own property back by breaking into my former room before the Gestapo would remove all of it? We would take that risk!

When Herbert and I headed back to my apartment in the Niebuhrstrasse 76, barely five weeks had elapsed since the "Gestapo Night." We rang the bell; nobody answered. Had all the former inhabitants been deported? And if that had happened, was it in revenge for my escape? Or had some of them gone to the early morning shift in their factory workplaces? Unanswerable questions, but they are still with me. I still had the key and opened the door carefully. All was quiet. We entered the hallway. A Gestapo seal was pasted over the lock of my room. Herbert removed it carefully, so that we could stick it back on after the completion of the intended mission: a break-in to recover my belongings. By the laws of the German Reich, all Jewish property was forfeited after deportation. My escape had put me into the category of people without rights. From that moment on, I had lost my German nationality, all property, my right to self-determination, and, though it was never said publicly, my right to self-preservation. I, as a person, as a citizen of Germany, had ceased to exist.

At the door of the apartment in the Niebuhrstrasse, I stood beside Herbert, my heart thumping, as he worked to open the lock of my former room with a lock pick. A sigh of relief, when the door jumped open suddenly! We discovered that the room was in total disarray, and the things most dear to me, presents from my mother, gone. My consternation grew when we discovered that two specific items I had hoped to recover were missing: one was the locked suitcase; the other, my address book and

correspondence, including photos. The drawer in which these
had been kept stood wide open and empty.

As far as my address book and correspondence were concerned, I could only hope that it did not contain any leads the
Gestapo could follow up. In addition to correspondence and addresses, all mementos were gone: the bundle of letters my
mother had returned to me on our last day together had disappeared along with all the photos of childhood, youth, and family
events. Not one photo of mother, father, brother, or grandmother was left. All mementos of the past I wanted to have and
to keep were scattered to the winds, or possibly intentionally
destroyed. Just as the Nazis destroyed us, so they also eradicated
any memory of us.

During the 1980s, when Herbert and I lived in Berlin for several years, I became aware that the Nazis had succeeded in obliterating our memory. I, naturally, met some of our Christian
neighbors, and established relationships with some of the members of the German-American Women's Club to which I belonged. I was struck by the astonishment I caused when they
discovered I was a former German Jew. It was as if they walked
around me to look for a cloven hoof, or a trait foreign to them:
my language had no foreign accent, my gesture, my manner,
and my appearance seemed recognizable to them. How could I
appear to be so average when they had learned that being Jewish
was being different? Then, at first timidly, they asked questions:
where had I lived in Germany, what was my Jewish upbringing,
what did it mean to be Jewish? Many of these questions were
answered by coincidence: a neighbor and I found out that she,
too, came from Wolfenbüttel. We had even gone to the same
school, though years apart, and had some of the same teachers.
As we chatted around a coffee table and the others listened, I
could sense that I had lost some of my "Jewish mystique." The
Hitler image of the "alien Jew" had been penetrated by a new
reality. The German-American Women's Club was different, and
had a more intellectually oriented international atmosphere. I
made friends with some of the members from the beginning, but
I knew of others there who had not shed their prejudice.

Looking around my room, I found that the Gestapo had taken
from it what they pleased. Gone, too, was the suitcase with the

initials C. B. that had led to questions by the SS men the night I
fled. During the five weeks of our hiding, I had not been able
to find out anything about the whereabouts of my friends, the
Bielschowskis. I did not know where they lived now in hiding.
What had been in their bags and knapsack was still lying dishev-
eled on my bed, but that suitcase, which they needed to support
their underground life, was gone: their belongings were lost to
them, stolen by the thieving underlings of the Gestapo. Their
greed was insatiable—a greed exhibited not only by these despi-
cable policemen, but by the top of the hierarchy. Reichmarschall
Hermann Göring, himself, was the mastermind of the looting,
pillaging, and expropriating that went on all over Europe, as
long as the fortunes of war were with them.

In their dealings with Jews, the Nazis' abysmal hatred had
joined with greed and led to universal robbery: they impoverished the Jewish community in the most rapacious way before
obliterating Jewish life. They impoverished my parents and destroyed my father's business. The supreme irony was that, after
having taken everything away, they still forced the Jews in the
Levetzowstrasse, before they were deported, to fill out a multi-
page list of everything they once owned. This document would
go to the State Financial Authority (*Landes Finanzamt*) which in
the proper legal form used it to confiscate their property for the
German Reich. In June 1994, Herbert found in the Berlin Landes-
archiv, in the files of the financial authorities deposited after the
war, the last document signed in their earthly life by my mother
and father on October 24, 1942.

Another weird example of the bureaucratic minds of these
"desk murderers" was that Herbert's name was listed among
"Communist" enemies of the Reich in the official Law Gazette
of the Government, of September 2, 1943. Since he was a student,
all he owned was the furniture in his room, his clothing, and his
books. Yet, by this notice, he was deprived of his property. No
mention was made that he had crossed the border into Switzerland in June 1943. It was all so demeaning that Herbert and I,
when the German Consulate offered to return German citizenship to us, of which the Nazis had deprived us, spontaneously
rejected the offer. We had found our peace in becoming American citizens.

These were sad moments spent in my room, as we tried to get my belongings out as quickly as possible. We were thieves in my own room! It was an act of defiance, a risk, that we did not want to extend a moment longer than necessary. We started packing whatever I might need into suitcases we had brought along for that purpose. Then we closed and locked the room and put the Gestapo seal back on the door as well as we could. We left as silently as we had come.

An incessant worry for me was the fate of my parents. Fears and doubts mingled with the uncertainty about where they might have been taken. The total secrecy with which the Nazis surrounded the "resettlement policy" was maddening for us. We did not have any means of penetrating this silence, any sources of inquiry, any rumors which could reveal the slightest hope about their fate.

From 1933 on, right after the Nazi seizure of power, we knew of two concentration camps in the Berlin area, Oranienburg and Sachsenhausen, and others farther south, such as Dachau and Buchenwald. The entrance doors to all of them proclaimed, in worked metal, the taunt, *Arbeit macht frei!* (Work sets free!), which, of course, was as false a pretense as ever existed. Everybody knew that behind their electrified cyclone fences horrible things were happening. The truth of these tortures and mistreatments were told by those who were arrested during Kristallnacht in 1938 and who were lucky enough to be dismissed after they had signed over their fortunes, and their families had brought proof that they would leave Germany within a short time. As terrible as this story of the concentration camps on German soil is, at least we knew of their existence and that some of those who were imprisoned in them had returned to the outside world to tell of their experience.

But in 1939, with the outbreak of the war, and in 1941, at the start of the "resettlement policy," we knew only that the deportation trains had gone to the East: the destination of the trains and the fate of the passengers were a blank in our imaginations. They took hold of our thoughts and would not be satisfied until we would learn the truth about their fate. We had only a few clues, which led us to believe that Eastern ghetto-towns were the recipients of this human cargo: towns like Warsaw, Lodz, Wilna, and Riga were well known to us as having large ghettoes. It seemed in keeping with Nazi theory that in order to "cleanse" the Deutsche Reich of all Jews—they called it *judenrein*—they had taken them and crammed them into already overcrowded and miserable conditions. Our thoughts turned around in circles to search for my parents: it was a repetitive effort that yielded no sign of hope.

It was at this time that I met my former husband. We ran into each other accidentally in the neighborhood of the Olivaer Platz, where I then lived in General Marcks's apartment. I was crossing the street and he, on his motorcycle, had stopped for the red light. We were surprised to see each other after such a long time and after my life had taken on such a different bent. He pushed his motorbike onto the curb, so that we could talk. In hushed tones I told him what had happened during the night of October 24. I knew that I could confide in him because he and his parents had been anti-Nazis. I was sure that this "inherited" attitude would not have changed. I had been right in my assumption. The events of war had also changed his life: he had been drafted into the military and had become a dispatch-rider, stationed, of all places, in Riga. When he mentioned Riga, it gave me a jolt. While he spoke, I had immediately established a possible connection to my parents. Was there a possibility that he could find out anything about deportation from Berlin to the Riga ghetto? Yes, he was willing to do what he could and would let me know. A few months later he called at Hella's: his report was negative. It seemed then that I would have to live with this nagging anxiety about my parents as a constant in my life.

A visit to Rheinsberg was one of the most absurd interludes during our life underground. During December, Hella Gorn made plans to visit this little town. If she had read the book that Kurt Tucholsky, a left-wing writer of the 1920s and 1930s, wrote about Rheinsberg I do not know. It was not Tucholsky's usual satire, unless he wanted to advocate "free love," but a straightforward romantic novel of young love and passion. It had become a bestseller, and many of the young women my age had become admirers of Rheinsberg. Rheinsberg was, and is, a little town to the north of Berlin and had been famous before. The novel merely added to its romantic appeal. King Frederick II, the hero and darling of Prussian history, had lived in a small summer palace in Rheinsberg, and ever since then the town was filled with memories of the flute-playing Prussian king. It had an aura of Prussian romanticism and attracted many visitors during the summer season.

Hella had planned the visit for the end of December. She had invited a small group of young Quakers and me to spend a few days there together: the highlight was to celebrate New Year's Eve together. Herbert was not invited to join the group: that was Hella's dictum. Understandably, during this time, my mind was not directed toward "having fun," especially not if I had to be with strangers worlds removed from what concerned me. Reluctantly, I agreed to the plan. When we arrived it was cold and gray. I did not see much of Rheinsberg's attractions, but at one point, a group of five or six people set out for a walk that turned into a weird experience for me. While we were walking in a loose group together, Hella suggested to me that I should leave Herbert and marry one of the young men in the group. She had already chosen one who, she said, was willing to marry me "in a blink of an eye." I could not believe that she had really said that to me! My expression must have shown my stupefaction. My next reaction was anger, but I knew that angry words would not prevail against her irrationality. In a matter-of-fact way, I explained to her that I would not separate from Herbert under any condition, and that her suggestion of marriage between a Christian young man and me was *Rassenschande* (a Nazi term for sexual relations with a non-Aryan) according to German law and would lead to imprisonment or worse were we to attempt it. I objected also to her repeated and undue intrusion into my life.

Of course, I was very well aware that I owed Hella gratitude for sheltering me, even if she exploited my dependent position. But in suggesting separation from Herbert and marriage to a Christian, she had gone beyond a definable line of what reasonable people could accept. Where had her unfounded hatred for Herbert taken her? For the life of me I could not understand her ill will. One glance at Herbert—before they had even exchanged greetings—had been the wellspring of her hatred: he bore a resemblance to a former boyfriend who had left her! An unfounded opinion not to be argued with. At this moment, in Rheinsberg, I began to resent her and even to fear her plans for our future.

I never saw Hella again after 1943, and for many years I did not know what had happened to her. Many years later we learned that she and Peter Heilmann had married after the war and settled in the East, then the German Democratic Republic, first known as the "Soviet-Occupied Zone," and later an independent Communist state. Without rhyme or reason, so Peter said, they were thrown into prison in the East. After they were set free, they divorced. Peter returned to West Berlin: when we met him in Berlin, after twenty-five years, he had remarried and was associated with the Evangelical Academy in West Berlin. Hella had stayed in the East and had died of cancer.

In the summer of 1994, when we got permission from the Swiss Government to look at our documents in the Swiss Archives in Bern, I found among my records Hella's passport, which she had given me as identification for the train trip from Berlin to Singen. We did not look similar but had the same eye and hair coloration and the same short hairstyle. We hoped that in the night train from Berlin to Singen the passport could serve as identification. I was grateful to her for giving me this expired passport, but in the end, I did not have to use it because I met with no identity checks on the train trip. Looking at her passport in the archives brought back many of the memories of this time and of her part in our fate and that of others: knowing of our contact in Switzerland, and using the connections we had established, Hella helped at least two other people to escape after we had left, Gert Ehrlich and Else Behrend-Rosenfeld, who wrote a book about her experiences as a Jewess in Germany, *Ich stand nicht allein* (I stood not alone).

The same Hella who helped these two persons and me grossly abused the mortal danger we were in by forcing me to submit to her will and by trying to betray Herbert. Our experience with her reveals our total vulnerability to such pathological whims. I am sorry that I cannot find another word for her contradictory behavior.

After German unification in 1989–90, when East German archives were opened, a Berlin newspaper reported that Peter

Heilmann had been an agent supplying the East German State Security Police, the Staats-Sicherheit, abbreviated "Stasi," with information to the very day this news appeared. Questioned by a reporter, Peter Heilmann insisted, according to the article, that he was proud of what he had done and would do it again. Even if he had been compelled to serve the Communist secret police to provide information, the informant's usual excuse that he was fighting fascism sounds rather hollow. Thinking of Peter and Hella makes me feel sad about these two German lives, thrown off balance by the Nazi terror that murdered Peter's father and landed them in another totalitarianism.

That day in Rheinsberg Hella and I continued our walk in silence, December 31, 1942, New Year's Eve, the night of Sylvester, ending the old year, which had brought on so much heartache. Since our flight Herbert and I lived at the edge of a precipice from which we could be hurled at any moment. Could we escape this vortex of destruction? What hope did we have of surviving as the new year began—even though I was determined to keep a small ray of hope alive in our infinitely dangerous situation? When we returned to our lodgings, I found a message from Herbert telling me that he had arrived in Rheinsberg and was waiting for me to join him. I could have cried with happiness; whereas before I had been so desperate, now I was on a roller coaster of feelings, and I liked what they did to me.

In a great rush, I left a note for Hella and Peter, informing them that I would spend the afternoon and evening with Herbert, and immediately set out to meet him. Herbert was in a small "bed and breakfast" place in a side street of Rheinsberg. It seemed to me that I ran all the way and ended in his arms breathlessly, being hugged and kissed and comforted, to which I responded in kind. We found happiness in each other and felt that nothing and nobody had the right to separate us. Both of us were determined to enjoy every minute we had together, at least the waning afternoon and evening of the old year and Sylvester night. We felt cooped up in his room; a restlessness had gotten hold of us, after Herbert had listened to my story of confrontation with Hella. We felt the need to act and to talk about our situation. Since we had met—more than three years before—we had always walked together, at first in the beautiful environment of Kladow. The mere action of walking together created a nearness we enjoyed; it released thoughts and brought Herbert out of his silences, at least to a degree, to talk more about himself and the difficulties every Jew during these terrible times was confronted with, but more so for a complex young man who had studied for the rabbinate, as Herbert had. It seemed that new thoughts formed on our walks, turning into unforeseen perspectives.

On this December day in Rheinsberg, we had new territory to explore and also the aim of finding a little pub or restaurant where we could spend the evening with each other, undisturbed, before we had to return to our separate hiding places—a return that, at this point, was hard to imagine.

What happened that day was surprisingly different from what we had anticipated. Our aimless walk through Rheinsberg with its tree-lined streets took us to a square with a rather large building on one side. On nearer inspection in the receding light of the winter afternoon, the building turned out to be a hotel. It looked like a comfortable hotel with its broad steps, a canopy with its name, and wide entrance door. Without any doubt, it was the hotel for the bourgeoisie of Rheinsberg. A sign over the entrance announced a New Year's Eve dinner for this evening. We stopped short, looking at the sign and then at each other with a question in our eyes. No doubt, both of us had the same thought: should we or shouldn't we? I looked intently at Herbert and, no question, there was a smile on his face, even a mischievous grin. He spontaneously took a step forward, halted, held out his hand for mine, and together we walked toward the hotel, up the steps and into the hotel lobby, into the "Lion's Den." I really do not know another word for it, nor can I give the feeling any other expression. We walked up to the reception desk and asked for a table for two for that night's dinner. "Yes," came the polite answer; "there is one." We paid for the dinner tickets and left. We had acted on a dare, and it had succeeded, at least so far. Had our behavior anything to do with the knowledge that "security" was to be found in the midst of the enemy? Or was there also a mixture of disproving their racial theories of "master race and underclass"? "Look," I could say to them "my self-respect was not diminished by your theories" and "you do not recognize me, walking among you." Was I triumphant, if only a little bit, because I knew a higher and older truth?

Later, when we returned to the hotel for dinner, we were led into a rotunda festooned with confetti and balloons, the festively laid out tables arranged around a dance floor. Our mood had changed abruptly: we wanted a good dinner, not a silly party; the mimicry would become unbearable even as play-acting. Absurdity could overwhelm us. A "total war" was throwing long and depressing shadows over the German future. Could it be that this crowd did not know anything of an encircled German army in Russia, or about defeat in North Africa? No, they did not know or did not want to know the reality. These people around us, were they the same ones who announced their losses on the battlefield "with pride" in giving their loved ones to the Fatherland?

Theoretically, and in hindsight, I know that wartime reinforces the search for that "reckless abandon," but I did not then, and do not now, think that this merrymaking crowd was searching for compensation. I felt that this was routine celebrating with a good conscience of average people, neither villains nor saints but fellow travelers and opportunists, the self-satisfied world that made Hitler possible.

As we sat in their midst and were not "found out," our original cockiness at being in the lair of the enemy, and not being found out, disappeared as spontaneously as it had come. I looked at Herbert and saw that the earlier mischievous smile had vanished from his face. Instead, there was a distant look in his eyes that reached far beyond the room. We got up and left the confetti-throwing crowd behind us, knowing that we would never again choose to be part of them.

The next day, we returned to Berlin to our separate hiding places. I returned to General Marcks's apartment in the Bregenzer Strasse with Hella. She never mentioned Rheinsberg or New Year's Eve, and I did not meet anyone from the Quaker group again. I cannot account for her change in attitude but was glad that all recollection of the day was suppressed, and that we could return to the routine we had established before.

To call it a routine is absurd; at best it was a routine of survival, in which certain tasks had to be done. Obtaining ration cards and food was one of our most important concerns. In addition, I had to maintain the story of being "a bombed out" (*ausgebombt*) person, and in that official status I was entitled to receive ration cards. To maintain this disguise, I had to keep in touch with some of our earlier contacts in Kladow, persons who had their own reasons to oppose the Nazi Regime (Seventh Day Adventists, neighbors of Polish descent), and they gave me what they could. We met usually halfway between Kladow and the city. Whatever I got, I shared with Herbert and Alma, General Marcks's housekeeper and cook. Later, when I became friendly with Alma and trusted her, I dropped the pretense of being bombed out and paid her a small sum, which I thought she deserved. Herbert's mother, too, who lived in Würzburg, sent food parcels, which were a great help to us.

Another pressing need for us was to get identification papers. If Herbert had no papers, the police might arrest and deport him at any time. To plan an escape to Switzerland without them was impossible. We had retained our circle of friends and tried to extend it. Up to this point, our search for papers had been fruitless, which was especially disheartening to me for Herbert's sake. I knew or assumed that life confined by restrictions would weigh heavily on him, though I never heard a complaint from him about it. On the contrary, he always showed a positive attitude, but I was worried about him.

Through the terrible events Jews had to endure, Jewish life in Germany was severely changed or disrupted. But I thought that the disruption affected Herbert more deeply, because, even in his young years, he had established intellectual interests, which became the determining factor in his life. He was considered one of the promising students at the Lehranstalt für die Wissenschaft des Judentums, and I knew that his teachers, including Rabbi Leo Baeck, had expected him to have an exceptional academic career. Suddenly his development and education had been interrupted by the Nazis. Now, like all Jews, he had to do forced labor. He was sent to Lankwitz (a southwest borough of Berlin) to be a streetcleaner, the right "punishment" for a young Jewish intellectual. This measure did not remove him entirely from his intellectual environment, for he could enjoy his reading and his books during his free time and keep limited contacts with his teachers. Our escape into the night had separated him entirely from his interests, however. It was not only a hunted life away from everything that was dear to him, but also a life without future and hope. How would he bear up under the added stress of the losses of his father and my parents? Might he become listless or even get sick, as he did, when he had to say the last good-bye to his father before deportation? Or might he repeat his volunteer offer to be deported with the congregation in which he had served not long ago? I had no answers to these questions, but they worried me, and I decided to ask Mr. Friedrich, the next time I met with him about the progress of the planned escape, and for information only he might have about the destination of our parents.

We knew that Herbert's father had been sent to the Warsaw ghetto, but the contact had stopped in June 1942, and we had heard nothing further from him. We also had no information about my parents, who had been taken to an unknown destination.

I believed, though, that there must be people in the Jewish congregation who would have known where they had been sent. As much as we tried, we were not able to get the slightest lead. Wherever we asked, we met walls of silence. It must have been a deeply guarded secret.

It was at this time, during the first half of January 1943, that Herbert told me about a dinner invitation he had received for the two of us from Friedrich Strindberg in Kladow.

Friedrich Strindberg was the son of August Strindberg, the Swedish writer. He had retained his Swedish nationality and was working as a journalist in Berlin for the *Berliner Illustrirte Zeitung*, the best-known illustrated weekly in Germany. He and his wife, a young Dutch woman, lived in Kladow, where my family had met them. They had offered Herbert a hiding place in their house after our stay in August's cellar had come to an end. Though, by mutual agreement, the arrangement with the Strindbergs had ended by this time, Herbert had kept in contact with them. We were surprised by the invitation, because they knew that I had to avoid being seen in Kladow for fear of being recognized. Assuming that they must have good reason to extend this invitation, we braved the journey, huddling on the upper deck of Bus No. 34 to Kladow on a dark January evening.

There, in his house in Kladow after dinner, Mr. Strindberg told us that in the conquered territories the Nazis had established extermination camps, surrounded by secrecy, where they were methodically gassing Jews. He said that his source was unassailable and asked us to keep this information secret.

We were stunned. I had no breath to say anything. The news came like a blow to my own life, and I tried to shrink away from it as far as I could to keep my sanity. But Mr. Strindberg, understanding our reaction, repeated that his information had been verified.

We said nothing for a long time, or so it seemed to me, rejecting this horror story. Then, under the influence of Strindberg's insistence, we began questioning the possibility, then slowly weighing the likelihood that these mass atrocities could be true. Admitting them for a second and shrinking from them became a process of twisted feelings and horror. Herbert finally burst out: "Strindberg, this is a mad story, I cannot believe it! You are deranged!"

I was so staggered by this unimaginable inhumanity that I did not know how to hold on to my feelings or how to express them. But then, from the back of my mind, I recalled having heard Hitler's strident voice in one of his speeches saying words to the same effect: "the extermination of the Jewish race in all of Europe. . . ." He had decreed the hatred of Jews as the mainstay of his policy from the beginning, and this piercing shrillness toward Jews had increased all along with his actions during the war years. Was it too far-fetched to think that Hitler wanted to do away with the Jews entirely? A sudden clarity hit me like a bolt of lightning. Suddenly I knew clearly that that was where my parents, Herbert's father, and all the others had been taken: to their death in the gas chambers! There would be no word from them and no hope of seeing any of them ever again. I could not express the horror I was feeling.

It was as if Strindberg's words had weights on them: they descended on me with a thud I could not bear. He had told us a truth that would be a steady companion and I knew it would never cease to exist. Life had shifted from its moorings, and it would stay askew. But I also knew that language has a limit beyond which it is difficult to go, even to describe the most heartrending events in our lives: a continuing crescendo of words and feelings is bound to appear trite.

Thus, during that month of January in 1943, our third month in hiding, we heard for the first time what was happening to the deported Jews in the conquered Eastern territories. We did not yet know that the fate of the Jews had been decided in Berlin at the Wannsee Conference on January 20, 1942, nor had we heard the name of the largest death factory, Auschwitz. Nor could we know that the massacre of six million Jews would become known to the world as the Holocaust or, in Hebrew, Shoa.

THE MURDER OF OUR PARENTS

What we heard from Strindberg on this evening for the first time has changed the consciousness of all Jews, including ours. Although the past grows more distant, the Holocaust looms larger in our memory. We have to accept the fact that, after their deportation, my parents and Herbert's father had been murdered. They did not return after the war. Now, we believed it to be our duty to find out as closely as possible what had happened to them and the many friends we lost in the Holocaust, no matter how discouraging our task might become: we felt compelled to know.

Herbert was the driving force behind the search. He had two goals: to find out the facts and to protect me, as much as he could, from learning the terrible details of the truth. He did not succeed entirely, because in our later New York intellectual environment what had happened in the camps was universally understood by Jews and Gentiles alike, and those terrible facts became increasingly part of New York political and literary culture. The war, and especially the Holocaust, were the cause of a deep hostility in American public life toward the Third Reich and anything German. Even we felt it, because we were German Jews.

During the war, in mid-1942, we knew that Herbert's father had been deported from Potsdam to the Warsaw ghetto. He had

written us that he had been confined in the Warsaw ghetto and
had sent a postal address. From Berlin and from Würzburg we
and Herbert's mother could send him small food parcels. A
short time later, he informed us that he would be sent farther
east. That was the last notice: after that we did not hear from
him anymore. After the war, Herbert learned that the date of his
last message coincided with the period when the Nazis began to
"liquidate" the Warsaw ghetto. We could not avoid reality any
longer and were forced to believe that Herbert's father had been
murdered in the gas chambers of Treblinka.

The fate of my own parents was long clouded by uncertaint-
ies. The first indication of their whereabouts emerged from the
Berlin transport lists: lists of all the transports from Berlin had
been compiled in which the number of people, date of leaving,
and destination were recorded. My parents were included in the
22nd *Ost-Transport*," leaving Berlin on October 26, 1942, with
791 Jews. Its destination was indicated only by the word *Osten*.
The previous transports had been routed to Riga. Afterward,
they were destined for Auschwitz, without exception.

To our next inquiry, directed to the Arolsen Tracing Center,
the answer was negative. Then Herbert placed a notice in three
German newspapers, searching for survivors of, or informants
on, the 22nd *Ost-Transport*. He received only vague answers and
requests for money. On a later trip to Berlin, in the 1970s, we
went to the *Kriminalgericht* in Berlin-Moabit, where a criminal
trial against Berlin Gestapo Beamte "Bovensiepen und Genos-
sen" (Berlin Secret Police Officers Bovensiepen and Others) was
conducted. For this trial, deportation lists for 35,000 Berlin Jews
had been assembled. Mr. Sczostak, the prosecuting state attorney, let Herbert examine the documents. They did not contain
anything about my parents, however. This was another disap-
pointing result. It seemed that for years our search had been
stymied. We met with a silence we could not penetrate and had
to assume that the transport had been moved in the direction of
Riga. Then it disappeared from the record. We never met anyone
who could give us so much as a hint of what happened to this
one transport. Nobody had ever returned, no survivor was ever
found—which forced us to conclude that the whole transport
had been destroyed within a short time after it left Berlin.

In Berlin in the 1980s, I got hold of a book by Ian Fleming, an English historian, who had traced the fate of the deportees of October 1942 in search of his own father. He confirmed that mass executions of German Jews had taken place in a forest near Riga. After reading Fleming's book, I had a stone, commemorating my parents, placed in the Wolfenbüttel cemetery, beside my uncle's grave, who died in Wolfenbüttel during deportation. It was as if they had rejoined the shadows of their former congregation.

After the fall of the Berlin Wall, Herbert was informed by the Riga Jewish Document Center that the transport of my parents was not mentioned in the lists of the Gestapo found in Riga. The archivist concluded that the transport had been stopped before reaching Riga, and that "the worst must be suspected" about the fate of the imprisoned 791 people. The many other steps Herbert and I took since the end of the War to trace the fate of my parents and this transport similarly ended in failure.

Finally, in mid-July 1999, we learned through an accidental encounter with a former colleague of Herbert's, Dr. Gertrud Schneider, of my parents' horrible death. She herself is a survivor of the Riga ghetto and since her liberation has done intensive research on the fate of the Jews in and around Riga and written books about it. Her story had a nightmarish quality—her voice betrayed it—and it is difficult to write it down. What I had been afraid of for many years now became a grim reality: during the fall of 1942, 40,000 Jews, mostly from Germany and France, were sent to the woods around Riga. Among them was the "22nd Osttransport," with 791 Jews from Berlin. They had been packed into regular passenger trains—not into cattle cars as was usual for Jewish transports. It must have given the prisoners a false sense of security and hid from them that the Nazi authorities intended an especially gruesome end for them: mass execution. Before arriving in the Riga ghetto, the train was diverted to a village named Salaspils. There, at the ramp, the transport was divided: fifty young men were sent to work in a sugar factory in Mitau, and a few more were detailed to help build the concentration camp Kaiserwald. (One, at most two, members of the work details survived.)

All the others—more than 700 people—were taken into the

woods to the killing grounds, where mass graves had been dug by Russian POWs. They were ordered to take off their clothes and step up to a wooden foot bridge leading to the mass graves, lie face down beside each other, or on top of each other, level upon level. Then they were killed by machine gun fire from the edge of the pit above them.

Mrs. Schneider told me that some of the mass graves have been overgrown now, but others remained sandy hollows where nothing will grow. In the mid-1990s, the woods of Salaspils became picnic grounds for the citizens of Riga. Our memorial stone for my parents in the Jewish cemetery in Wolfenbüttel remains the last memento to their life and death.

In 1984, the surviving remnants of the Jewish congregation of Wolfenbüttel met in the cemetery and unveiled a memorial plaque for the nineteen Jewish Families who had been murdered in the Holocaust. Rabbi Brandt (Hannover) conducted a short memorial service. Herbert and I return to the cemetery in Wolfenbüttel whenever we visit Europe and leave the traditional small stones on our family's tombstones. Herbert says kaddish, suggesting peace for our beloved, where there can be no peace. When we leave, we lock the gate and return the key to a neighbor. But the memory of the horrible cruelty my parents had to suffer in their last hours will haunt me for the rest of my life.

ESCAPE PLANS TO SWITZERLAND

During the month of January 1943, I met with Mr. Friedrich from the Red Cross. The news Mr. Strindberg had confronted us with was at once so real and yet so unbelievable—could human beings really do this to other human beings?—that I decided to ask Mr. Friedrich if he believed that the deliberate extermination of Jews was really taking place in the East. His answer avoided a direct confirmation. He repeated instead his earlier belief that the Nazis, as victory eluded them, would be more determined than ever to deport the Jews from Germany to an unknown destination. He explained to me that he had just come back from his home leave in Switzerland and, during his stay there, had impressed on my uncle the urgency to get us out of Germany as fast as possible.

It is clear to me now, in hindsight, that Mr. Friedrich must have been better informed than most: as an employee of the International Red Cross he knew about the course of the war. He had to deal with soldiers and prisoners of war, and he read Swiss newspapers, two of which, the *Thurgauer Zeitung* (in October 1942) and the widely read *Neue Züricher Zeitung* (on May 9, 1943) had commented on statements made by Hitler and Goebbels that in their opinion "confirmed openly—even with absolute clarity—the eradication of the Jews, no matter how the war would end." By stressing his earlier warning, Mr. Friedrich, too, seemed to recognize the extreme danger we and all others were in, but he avoided the angry abruptness of Mr. Strindberg's words.

After having carefully turned the conversation away from my question, he asked me to sit for a snapshot that he was to send to my uncle to hand over to the border guide at the appropriate moment in the future, at a still-to-be-determined meeting place. When Mr. Friedrich showed the picture to me, I was appalled by what I saw: there was no light in my eyes, and dark shadows threw a gloom over my face. The photo was not what I had expected. I always had thought of myself as being an open and friendly person, and I believed that these traits would be reflected in my face, as they always had been. Those characteristics had simply vanished. It was like looking at a strange person. I silently handed the picture back to him.

I was about to leave Mr. Friedrich when he indicated that he had another concern he wanted to discuss: he told me that as a representative of the Red Cross he was approached by a lady who was willing to assist anybody who was in need of such help, "excluding giving anybody shelter." He continued that he had formed a favorable impression of her and immediately thought that Herbert and I could benefit from such an offer of help. If I agreed, he would set up an appointment for us to meet. When Mr. Friedrich first mentioned this offer of assistance, I was confused about what this unknown person could do to alleviate our situation if she could not help me get away from Hella. I realized that it would be impolite toward Mr. Friedrich to reject this kind offer and stupid, too, because in our situation we should be grateful for any assistance offered. I could not foresee then what a crucial role this person—Mrs. Meier—would play in our rescue. Of course, I agreed to meet this lady.

On one of the following afternoons, Mrs. Meier and I met in the Taubertstrasse, one of the quiet side streets of Grunewald where she lived. At first, it felt a little awkward meeting a stranger who knew so much about me. As she introduced herself, I first thought that her name, Meier, was only a cover name. This name, and that she had come from Soest in Westphalia, was all I would know about her for the next forty years; her first name was never mentioned.

As we met and shook hands, I looked at her inquisitively, and she directed a searching glance at me. I estimated her to be in her middle fifties. She was of medium height, her gestures energetic, and she was well dressed, all in black. She did not strike me as a person paying too much attention to her appearance. I thought it incongruous that she wore a coquettish hat with a little half-veil attached to it. With a smile, we overcame our initial embarrassment, and she invited me up to her apartment. She proceeded with an eagerness that baffled me, or was it only her vivacity that produced the impression of eagerness? It felt almost as if she wanted to prove to me that she was trustworthy and that her apartment should help to reinforce this impression. Or did I misunderstand her motivation? (It was not until six months later that I found out that she was helping another Jewish woman—hiding and helping her to escape!) As we sat down to have tea, I had enough time to take notice of the surroundings: it was a luxurious apartment with a certain bourgeois solidity. As we sat and continued to talk, my confidence in her grew. She explained to me how she had become acquainted with the Jewish fate in these Nazi years.

She had had Jewish neighbors who owned and managed a "pension" for Jews. She was friendly with them and had met some of their guests, many of whom had come to Berlin to shorten their wait for a visa for emigration. Often, she had allowed them to use her telephone—because Jews were no longer allowed to own telephones, and in this way she and her husband had become familiar with all the heartbreaking stories of the people they met. She also knew what it meant in personal tragedy not to receive a visa for emigration. She explained her personal reason for becoming involved in trying to help: she had been widowed recently and felt that she should continue what she and her husband had started together. She was deeply religious, a devout Catholic who took her Christian beliefs seriously. Her three sons were serving in the German Army, but added to the usual worry about their welfare during wartime, it was a special fear for one of them. This son, as a convinced believer in Hitler, had a high position in the Waffen SS and could possibly be "involved in inhumanities against the Jews." Although she chose a more genteel word to describe the utter cruelties committed by the SS, she struck me as being deeply involved. Her conscience would not allow her to bear this guilt without trying to lessen it. Her penance was helping Jewish men and women in need to the best of her ability, and she kept her promise. When we said good-bye to each other, it was with the assurance that we would stay in contact through Mr. Friedrich.

If the winter of 1942–43 was a particularly cold one or not, I do not remember anymore, but I do recall that I became sick with a chest cold. Realizing that I needed medical advice, I turned to Dr. Walter Blank, whom I had consulted earlier, after Dr. Steinitz in Kladow had given up his practice. Exactly when I originally met Dr. Blank, I do not recall. It probably was in 1938 or 1939, when the violence of Kristallnacht took place—the night in which the SA and SS troops had burned the synagogues, smashed the remaining Jewish storefronts, looted or destroyed them, and sent many thousands of Jewish men to concentration camps. They freed them only when they submitted proof of an imminent emigration. Thereafter, even the most optimistic Jew despaired of living in Germany under Nazi rule with a modicum of toleration. That night's violence unleashed a frantic search for a way—any way—out. Whenever and wherever Jews met, the conversations started and ended with inquiries into the fastest ways of leaving Germany, the country of their birth. It had turned into enemy country, where no one was safe any longer.

After Kristallnacht, Jews led a diminished life, and tensions were high and needed release in whatever way possible. I became aware of this when I watched the circle of friends of Uncle Ernst and Aunt Hedi playing bridge in their apartment. The game of bridge had developed into a regular fad and attracted many aficionados who took it quite seriously. As a pastime, it had spread among Jews in Berlin who were forced to play the deadly serious game of waiting: waiting to get a number from the U.S. Consulate, waiting to be called by a consul, waiting to prepare additional papers, waiting for a ship's passage, waiting. Possibilities and hopes were discussed endlessly, and the game of bridge was a wonderful way to get together and to let thoughts wander into other channels than the sheer endless preoccupation with *Auswanderung* (emigration).

On one of these bridge afternoons, I met Dr. Blank and his friend, Dr. Rudolf Caspary. I did not understand anything of their card game, but their conversation attracted me. There was a lot of banter between them: it was obvious that they had not lost their sense of humor. But there was also a serious side. It appeared to me that Dr. Caspary was better able to cope intellectually and had a greater emotional distance from our common worries. He impressed me greatly by his way of putting things into perspective.

But between these parties and my time in hiding lay years. I knew Dr. Blank and his wife quite well: in the earlier years, they, too, had sometimes been guests in Kladow. I had been Dr. Blank's patient before, and did not hesitate to consult him again. He was still at his old address but was allowed to see only Jewish patients. It was pleasant to meet him again, and he very amiably offered his help, as I had hoped he would. After the examination we sat together like old friends and talked of what had happened to us, to my parents, and what was happening now all around us. Dr. Blank was a very good listener. He, too, had a certain detachment. I did not know if this was because of his experiences as a physician, or because he had overcome a tough challenge when he had poliomyelitis as a young man. He walked with a limp, and his face often looked drawn.

When I told him of our developing plans to escape to Switzerland, which might hinge on the possibility of finding identification papers for Herbert, he said to let him know when I had a firm escape plan. I looked at him questioningly. "Yes," he said,

"I believe that Caspary can do something to help Herbert in such a clear-cut situation." How often I asked him, and how often Dr. Blank had to repeat his answer, I cannot say anymore. I promised not to tell anybody except Herbert and left in a state of single-minded happiness, and took myself to bed with hot compresses and lemon juice and dreaming that Herbert and I would be free.

A few days later, my chest cold gone, I met Herbert and told him of Dr. Blank's wonderful news. There was a glow on his face as we walked arm in arm around the Berlin zoo. What a difference it makes to have a future!

During this time of hiding, Herbert and I had developed the rule that each of us would know in advance where the other would be. It was just a precautionary tactic but it created a feeling of safety, which was imaginary, as we well knew, because, if anything were to happen, we could not help each other. But neither of us dwelled on such morbid feelings: we trusted our luck. One afternoon when I visited Putto, whose story I have already told, I got a telephone call from Herbert that was unusual, because I did not expect a call from him at that hour. When I listened to what had happened to him, I became alarmed because what he reported sounded very cryptic: he "had run from an apartment, had jumped several staircases, run against a tree, and lost his glasses." I was shaken because it became clear to me that he had escaped by the skin of his teeth from a dangerous situation. What exactly had happened I did not know until I met him the next day. It was then that he told me that he ran into a Gestapo trap while visiting Willi Mayer. The door was opened by a young Gestapo man, who led him into the apartment where several "bedraggled people" were seated; Willi Mayer was not among them. I am not sure when Herbert recognized that this was a Gestapo dragnet. He was accompanied back to the entrance hall and asked to show his identification papers. By a ruse, he distracted the two Gestapo men for a fraction of a second, took a step toward the entrance door, tore it open, ran down the stairwell, jumped over the railing on the landing of the next floor, repeating this maneuver, more jumping than running, until he was out of the house and in the darkness of the street. He did not stop running until he bumped into a tree in Leibnizstrasse and lost his glasses.

As I listened to Herbert with deep alarm about his narrow escape, I became ecstatically happy: for now he was safe. But in the next moment I was hit—as though with a sudden blow to the body—with the realization that Willi Mayer must have been caught in the very situation from which Herbert had escaped. He could not have had any warning and must have walked straight into the Gestapo trap. In a few days, he would be on one of the cattle cars, used to deport Jews, rolling toward the East. We now know what that meant. I cannot express the feelings that overcame me at that moment: anger and hatred for the senseless killing of innocent and helpless people, and mourning for Willi Mayer. For the entire year we had worked together, he had picked me up every morning to make the long trip to the factory together. We walked together to Bahnhof Charlottenburg, where we took the elevated railway. Wearing the "Jude" patch, we had to stand the entire trip and were not allowed to talk to anyone. The trip from Bahnhof Charlottenburg to the Köpenicker Strasse, from West to East Berlin, lasted about an hour. For Willi Mayer it was the gentleman-like manner not to let a young lady travel alone, unprotected in a possibly threatening situation.

Every morning, in the pre-dawn hours he indicated his presence by whistling. He invariably chose one of two melodies. One tune was "Ich hatt' einen Kameraden, einen bess'ren find'st Du nicht" or "Morgenrot, Morgenrot, leuchtest mir zum frühen Tod." The sound of whistling floated up to me loud and clear, and I even remember that the last note was drawn out, a little trill added. I do not know why he chose two sad German soldier's songs, because Willi was a "hail-fellow-well-met" person; seriousness was not a word in his dictionary. His attitude was positive, even cocky at times. It felt good to be with him. I considered him, as his whistling indicated, to be my comrade-in-arms, my buddy. He had chosen these tunes wisely: they were appropriate for our lives on the edge. I remember them as being symbolic for these haunted times and they remain one with the memories I retain of Willi Mayer. After that day in winter 1943, he was never heard from again. It is still difficult for me to imagine that Willi was one of the many friends walking up the green hill, never to return.

It must have been at the same time that I made a new attempt to break away from Hella Gorn, but in vain. It only brought out a worse and unanticipated side of her character. When I called her office from one of the public phones at the U-Bahnhof Wittenbergplatz to tell her of my intention to leave, she said: "If you leave, I shall give your name to the Gestapo." I desisted but also knew from then on that she would use any means—spiteful and treacherous—to get her way. These—her—words were not just empty threats, as we learned after the war from Klix, whom she tried to instigate into giving us away.

On February 27, 1943—we will never forget that date—in the early morning hours, trucks pulled up at all factories where Jews were working. Robert Kempner, one of the prosecutors in the Berlin Gestapo case and a friend of ours, described it in *Gegenwart im Rückblick*, a book that Herbert co-edited: "Like shock troops, SS men, reinforced by units of the Leibstandarte Adolf Hitler" marched into the armaments factories and arrested the Jewish laborers. The victims were taken to several collection points and were guarded by SS units to isolate them from the outside world.

Nearly 10,000 Jews were rounded up during this raid. Shortly after these mass arrests, "six transports were leaving Berlin in freight-trains: the first one on March 1, and the other five followed during the month of March. They were numbered from 30 to 35, the exact date when they left was given, they were labeled *Ost Transport*, the destination was Auschwitz."

We heard the news from Herbert's friend Lutz Ehrlich. His mother was caught in this raid. He tried desperately to establish contact with her but could not even find out where they had taken her. Mrs. Ehrlich's brave attempt to feign suicide had saved her life once, but so many of our parents' generation were reluctant to imagine that "their country" had planned a murderous death for them. It was beyond their—or anybody's—imagination. How could it not have been so?

In my mind I could see the entrance to the factory of the Köpenicker Strasse, where I had worked. I thought of all the terrible scenes that must have taken place when my former co-workers came for the morning shift and realized that there was no escape from the waiting trucks and the SS men. Might Mr. Parlo have warned some of them as he had warned me? I shall never know.

In this atmosphere, it became almost impossible for me to keep alive any hope for survival and believe any longer in the postponement of our redemption, as we always had done. The German Jewish community was finally destroyed beyond denial and illusions. The German airwaves, too, were full of war news and *Sondermeldungen* (special news bulletins) accompanied by trumpets heralding great victories. Their sound was persuasive: they droned from every living room and every public place. Even when the war turned against the Germans, as it had recently, propaganda changed a retreat into an outflanking maneuver or an encirclement, as in Stalingrad, into tales of unsurpassed bravery. Political speeches at that time added a heretofore never heard shrillness to an already overheated emotional environment. On February 18, 1943, Propaganda Minister Goebbels gave a blatantly barbaric speech on "Total War" in the Sportpalast in Berlin. He asked the assembled brown cadres if they were willing to fight a total war with every ounce of their strength, to pledge a new allegiance to the Führer, to follow him into "final victory [*Endsieg*] or death"; the masses roared their approval to the rafters, and I heard them: the Germans, once more gave their stamp of approval to Hitler and chained themselves to him, come what may!

After the passage of more than fifty years, it is difficult to assign a definite time to the events that happened in our underground life. Still, they had a certain sequence, and carried with them such uncommon freight of emotions and danger that usually dormant feelings rushed to the fore and became unforgettable.

I believe that it was in February or March 1943 that the determining event of our underground life took place. It would mean the end of our hiding in Germany. A letter arrived from Ludwig in which he announced that he had found somebody to accompany us across the Swiss border. In order to avoid any error or mishap, he had laid out all the details we had to observe in order to succeed.

Our meeting place would be in Singen am Hohentwiel, a

larger town within a few miles of the border. The meeting place would be before the Singen post office, at precisely five o'clock in the afternoon. The day of the meeting should be a Saturday, possibly just before a holiday, to facilitate traveling from Berlin to Singen when the trains would be crowded. The border crossing the next day would be disguised as a Sunday afternoon walk. There would be two guides: the guide expecting us at the post office in Singen would approach us with my picture in his hand and would move on in order to leave the border area—especially the center of town, train station, and post office—promptly, so as not to arouse attention. We were to follow the guide who would be riding a bicycle, but we were not to walk directly behind him, especially when we had to traverse a wooded terrain. After walking for approximately twenty minutes, we would reach the next village, Gottmadingen, where the guide would indicate the house we should enter. This was the house of our second guide. We would be expected and would spend the night there. The man in Gottmadingen would have all responsibility from then on. He would be the one who would take us to the border early on Sunday afternoon and show us the direct path leading into Switzerland. This area, too, would be wooded, where the German and Swiss borders entwined sometimes, but we could trust our guide implicitly, as far as both his knowledge of the terrain and his character were concerned. Once in Swiss territory, we were to keep to the path indicated and shortly thereafter would meet another man waiting for us. He had been posted to lead us further into Switzerland, which was a precautionary measure to avoid being returned to Germany by the Swiss authorities. (The Swiss policy of refusing entry to refugees had prevailed until a short time before, as Jews were trying to escape from Vichy France after the German army had occupied it. Many had been rejected and been turned back across the border.) The letter continued: "If you are detected by a Swiss Border Guard and questioned by him, you should tell him that your life is endangered in Germany, that your family was annihilated and that if you want to send us back, shoot us first."

Dear Janie, do you understand the emotions that gripped me at that moment? It was as if a *Zauberberg* (a magic mountain) had opened and let two people walk in: there was a way out for the two of us! For Mr. Friedrich it was a success, too, because it was at his insistence that Ludwig had attempted to find a way and he had finally succeeded.

In his competent way, Mr. Friedrich started immediately to handle all the organizational matters. The first step was to get "official identification papers"—in which, however, regrettably, he would be unable to assist us. I told him of the possibility of getting valid military papers for Herbert. I do not remember any longer if I mentioned Dr. Blank's or Dr. Caspary's name to Mr. Friedrich. In hindsight, I wished that I had done so: it might have opened our route of escape to Dr. Blank, his family, and Dr. Caspary when they needed it. Mr. Friedrich suggested that I should cross the border on May 1, 1943. This date would meet the requirements set forth in the letter: it was a Sunday and a holiday, the day of the old May Day celebration. The Nazis had taken it over from the Socialists, and it was now a flag-waving hullabaloo for patriotic bureaucrats. It also was a spring day; a Sunday afternoon walk would be a pleasant pastime. Those few points settled, I left Mr. Friedrich in the best of moods.

When I informed Herbert about the letter, he was impressed, once he understood the radical turn this meant for our situation. Our redemption had moved a giant step closer.

After having told Herbert and Lutz—whom we had included in our plans, when he had not succeeded with his own, such as swimming the Rhine River in Herlingen—I also took the news to Hella and informed her about the escape plan, which I could not keep a secret from her anyway. She had an unexpected reaction: she offered me her recently expired passport as an identification paper. It had a black-and-white photo: the resemblance was not great, but dark hair and eyes and short hairdo might be enough for identification papers in a dark (black-out) train at night. I was very grateful to her. It is difficult to determine the risk she ran in giving me the passport: she might have claimed to have lost it. Anyway, I did not have the occasion to use it: there was no police control of our papers during our journey. It now rests with other records of ours in the file in the Bundes Archiv der Schweizer Eidgenossenschaft (Swiss federal archives in Bern).

The task of informing Dr. Blank and Dr. Caspary was a pleasant one. The meeting took place in Dr. Blank's apartment. While I was reading them the letter, I noticed that their expressions changed from doubt to intense interest to enthusiastic acceptance. It was evident that both men recognized that this was a solidly worked-out plan—at least as safe as any such plan could be—and that it might provide passage to freedom. As they were aware, its success depended on getting proper identification papers for Herbert. I believed that if it were in Dr. Caspary's power to obtain such documents he would try to do so. I waited for his word which would decide the feasibility of the plan. When his answer came, it was positive and succinct. All he said was: "Contact me in four weeks!" The brevity of his response sought to avoid any expression of gratitude. I left shortly thereafter with a wonderful sensation that we had taken a further step into the future.

But it was too early to celebrate the future: the plan suddenly went askew. Mr. Friedrich received a message from Switzerland that the guides refused to take a young man across the border. They assumed, and rightly so, that young, able-bodied men were supposed to serve in the army, without exception. This had been so since the beginning of the war, but the urgency of doing military service had increased since Propaganda Minister Goebbels had asked in his speech "Wollt Ihr den totalen Krieg?" and the answer was given with enthusiasm. Resisters or deserters would be executed: he had threatened that the Military Police would find them out. Under such threats, our guides in Singen would not tackle such a dangerous case. They knew that a young Jewish man could not possibly be in possession of the right documents. If he would be apprehended and interrogated, his escape plans to Switzerland could mean enormous danger for them, too.

An additional danger in this situation was that Allied prisoners of war—English or American flyers shot down over Germany—sometimes escaped from their prisoner of war camps and tried to flee to Switzerland. There was a built-in double risk: and we knew trains and streets leading to the border were tightly guarded by SS with shepherd dogs, and the border itself was closed off with barbed wire at many spots. For these reasons, the guides did not want to be part of such a risky situation.

They also said that they did not wish to meet any person except me at the meeting place in Singen.

When Mr. Friedrich told me about the changed plan, and I understood their refusal to have Herbert included, I was heartbroken and told Mr. Friedrich that I would not go without Herbert. I reminded him that from the beginning of our talks I had stressed that all escape plans had to include Herbert. I suffered guilt feelings that my precipitate escape in October 1942 had endangered Herbert's life and that it had been my fault that he had been thrown into "that stream from which no escape is possible." Shortly after our escape from the Gestapo at night, his mother said to me, "You are the misfortune of my son!" ("Sie sind das Unglück meines Sohnes!")—a remark not easily forgotten, but perhaps understandable for a mother who had just lost her husband to the same terrible fate, the "Jewish" fate.

But it was not just that I had made a promise and wanted to keep it. Who wants to save one's own life if one has to give up the only person one loves? I was not ready to do that, and I told Mr. Friedrich so. In our former conversations, Mr. Friedrich had been invariably polite, and he was so now: I had always been at liberty to accept or reject his advice, but in this conversation he used sharper arguments and pressed home his point of view. Apparently, he had anticipated my arguments and was ready for them.

He told me that the May 1 appointment still stood and that Mrs. Meier was ready to accompany me to the border. All preparations for the trip would be in her hands, so that I did not have to bother with tickets or anything else connected with the journey. He asked me how I would feel if that date passed and all efforts on my behalf would have been in vain because I had refused to go. Also, did I think that my staying could be of further assistance to Herbert? He added that, by May 1, I might be able to convince the guides that Herbert and his friend Lutz would be in possession of the necessary documents to make the trip to the border without endangering themselves or anybody else. I might therefore be able to alleviate their fears. His last argument hit me like a barb, because I felt, that there was truth in it. He said, "If you don't go, nobody else will, but if you go, others may follow you!" Herbert, too, supported Mr. Friedrich strongly, so I was under pressure from both sides, and I did not know how to withstand this onslaught on my emotions. I was in a predicament I did not know how to resolve and felt very unhappy. After I made the decision to go by myself, I felt even more unhappy. Even when I was "safely" in Switzerland, this sense of loss did not leave me. Once found, happiness is hard to give up! I had this vision of standing alone at the edge of a lake seeing all my friends drown. The Red Sea had returned!

A few weeks later, Dr. Caspary handed me a letter when we met again in Dr. Blank's house. There was a smile on his face, and I knew that he was to give me a wonderful present. I, too, smiled up at him and let the envelope rest on my palm before opening it. There were two postcard-sized identification papers in it on shiny gray linen paper. At first, they did not look impressive, but then I saw the heading on them saying in bold black print: Heeres- und Bewaffnungsamt Speer (armament authority directed by Albert Speer, the famous technocrat). They were blanks: no picture, no signature, and no rank of employment. All the details were to be filled in and matched to a military pass that Ossi, Herbert's present host, a worker in the giant Borsig factory, had somehow acquired for Herbert. Before this, we had already talked to our friend Wanda with the "snap-fastener-machine" and were sure that she could attach the photos and would be glad to be of help to us. Receiving these documents made it easier for me to leave and meet the guides in Singen. I hoped that the obstacles they had foreseen could thus be overcome, as Mr. Friedrich had said.

There is very little I can write about Dr. Caspary's life and nothing about his person. All I knew about him I had heard from my uncle and aunt in whose house I had met him as a friend of theirs. They had told me that he had been a state district attorney, and some years before had been a junior prosecuting attorney in the Barmat-Kutisker trial, a notorious corruption case involving two financiers, which had attracted notice in German nationalist circles. His reputation as a conservative had been established then, but nobody knew if any ties to such a group had existed then, or, if so, whether those ties had continued until 1943.

That Dr. Caspary was able to give me two blank identification

papers from a major ministry certainly suggests that he had
maintained contact with influential civil servants after he had
been dismissed from his position in 1933. This assumption
might be confirmed by a remark he made to me in passing,
sometime during this period, that he "felt protected."

Many years after the war, we learned that he had received
these identification cards from a high civil servant who had been
actively engaged in resisting from within the system. He was
Werner Keller, about whose activities we heard only ten years
after his death. Because Mr. Keller refused to commit his experiences to writing, and later lived in Switzerland, he remains a
shadowy figure among German wartime resisters. He was arrested in February 1945, brought to the military prison in Tor-
gau, and barely escaped being executed for high treason: he had
been caught operating two radio-transmitters directed to the
United States, appealing for a separate peace, to make a common front with Germany against the Soviet Union, which was,
of course, an unrealistic expectation.

There is reason to believe that Dr. Caspary and Mr. Keller
knew each other from their service in the Berlin Kammergericht.
Werner Keller started his career there when Rudolf Caspary was
dismissed in 1933, after having served there for several years.
The Stauffenberg Memorial in Berlin allowed Herbert to see the
files during the summer of 1994, when we also met Mr. Keller's
daughter, a Berlin gynecologist. We were happy to meet one
member of his family, to express our gratitude for his help.

Rudolf Caspary's trust in the "protection" he had mentioned
to me was sadly misplaced. After the war, we learned that he
had been deported. In the German Federal Gedenkbuch listing
all Jewish dead in the concentration camps, the entry for Dr.
Caspary reads: *"Auschwitz, verschollen"*—fate unknown. The
Gedenkbuch for Berlin Jews lists "Dr. Walter Blank, geb. 31.12.94
Hannover. Susi Blank née Hammerschlag geb.1.11.1904, Lise-
lotte geb. Berlin 11.1929 und Rita geb.8.9.1930 in Berlin deported
on May 17, 1943 to Auschwitz, verschollen."

At no time can I forget what these two men did for us: their
willingness to help saved Herbert's and his friend's lives. But
that is not enough to say in their memory: both played important
roles in German society: one as a jurist and the other as a doctor.

Both were raised in a once honorable German tradition and followed high ethical standards. Both were freedom-loving individuals. Their persecution, their imprisonment, and their murders are deeds of inhumanity to be mourned for all time.

The date of my leaving Berlin was approaching fast; it was set for April 29, 1943, to be in time for the meeting in Singen on the next day at five o'clock. This day of leave taking had and still has an emotional impact on me. Every year, when the date approaches, I think of it, and in my mind, add one year to the count. So far, the count stands at fifty years!

I had promised myself not to go without Herbert and had assured him innumerable times that I would not leave without him. Still, here I was at the Anhalter Bahnhof—today only three arched pillars are left to tell you where the station once stood; a ruin and memento of the destruction of World War II. There was no denying that I was going, but I was not ready to go. I just did not comprehend that I could leave this man who had turned my life around, who had given me a new sense of life and strength. But, at this particular moment, on the platform of the Bahnhof—where everything was open—it would have been dangerous for both of us if I were to show my feelings. I knew that it would end with my crying, creating a scene, the "forbidden thing" to do: to draw attention to oneself. And, besides, we had been over the arguments back and forth, for going and against going, and Herbert had prevailed: I had to go!

Finally, I climbed up the steps into the train, which was to take me to Singen. I stood at the window of the train looking down at Herbert. He looked up at me with an expression that I took for forced optimism. The only sign of irritation—or embarrassment—that I detected was that he turned his hat, a gray felt hat, with both his hands. His face, though, expressed a "chin up" optimism, and his last words to me were: "Good-bye, until we see each other soon again!"

At this moment, I did not believe in a successful border-crossing: only together with Herbert could I have the courage to do something that daring. Alone, I felt that all my energy had evaporated. I could not imagine my future without him. How would I cope coming out of a world where Jews were deliberately murdered and where I had been hiding to escape this fate? How would it feel to step into a normal world: could the nightmares be banned from my thoughts? How would it feel to be able to trust again? I believed fervently that there were people around the world, in Switzerland, England, and the United States, believed in the inviolable rights of a person. But to me, at that moment, this "sane world," *die heile Welt*, was light years removed. They would meet me with open arms and offers of help—especially my aunt and uncle in Lausanne—but would they also understand what was going on in Germany at this time and that I might not be able to shake this memory, especially not as long as Herbert was in the grip of "that evil"?

As the train started moving, Herbert waved to me with his hat in slow motion. I tried to hold on to him with my eyes, then he was gone. I took a few moments to get hold of myself and then stepped into the compartment, where Mrs. Meier was seated, waiting for me. It was a second-class compartment, used in every express train (D-Zug) at that time in Germany. An express car had about twelve such closed-off compartments, which one entered from the corridor through a sliding door. Each compartment had eight seats, four on each side. Each seat on the train was numbered: a system that allowed seats to be reserved in advance. Mrs. Meier had done so, and had also bought the tickets well in advance, anticipating difficulties with crowded trains during wartime. My seat was near the window, farthest away from the door. Mrs. Meier was seated next to me, as if to protect me from prying eyes.

I apologized for letting her wait. She understood without words. There was not much that we could say to each other: every seat was occupied, and our remarks could be heard by everybody. Anyway, she had long planned the details for this journey. We would pretend that I was the fiancée of her youngest son, a soldier, who had been wounded and had been sent to the Lazarett (hospital) in Singen. We were on an urgent visit to see him in the hospital. We hoped it sounded believable should we ever be asked. The train was overcrowded and dimly lighted: the ticket control was only perfunctory. There were no police controls. I leaned back into my corner, occupied with my own thoughts. In the early dawn hours, when the train sped through Würzburg, Herbert's hometown, all the happy might-havebeens crowded my memory. During the morning hours, the train arrived in Stuttgart, where we had to change. The connecting train was already on the opposite tracks: people were crowding at the entrances, attempting to board it; others, mostly soldiers, were trying to climb through the windows. They hung there like grapes.

Here was our first difficulty! We knew that we could not penetrate through this solid phalanx of people and knew, too, that we had to be on this train to keep my appointment in Singen that afternoon. Missing it would keep us from being in time; it might destroy all our plans. We stood with a small group of people on the platform, not knowing what to do, when the conductor—blue uniform, red bandolier—showed up, ready to enter his compartment at the front of the train, right behind the engine. He noticed our plight and invited us to use his compartment. This was a stroke of luck: we had seats on the train and did not encounter any police or Gestapo controls.

Soon, a little group traveling together was in the middle of a lively conversation. It turned to air raids on West German towns. I remember hearing, "part of Düsseldorf is burning," and the apprehension was expressed that these attacks might increase and extend over larger areas. I kept out of this discussion entirely and was surprised that this theme was so openly discussed, because the spreading of negative war news was strictly "forbidden." The discussion was not an open critique of the war, but the discussion did contain the seeds.

At noon, the train arrived in Singen. I offered a woman my help in carrying her suitcase. As I did so, I was suddenly asked by a uniformed customs officer what I was doing. I recognized with a jolt that I had gotten myself into a situation that had attracted unwanted attention. I answered calmly, "Just to help," put down the suitcase, turned toward Mrs. Meier, and jointly we left the station.

Mrs. Meier's pretense of the hospital visit in Singen not only served as a basis for our going to Singen, but also helped us avoid the center of town during the afternoon hours. Singen was in "border territory" and had more than enough customs and Gestapo controls keeping a sharp eye out for any strangers aimlessly walking about. We had several hours to while away until it was time to meet the guide at five o'clock. We walked to the hospital, and once we were there, Mrs. Meier busied herself at the information desk to locate the whereabouts of her son and kept the hospital staff busy for a while. Since it was a "make-believe" story, there was, of course, no result.

Her errand completed, she joined me in the lobby of the hospital, carrying cups of hot tea to complement our lunch, sandwiches, which she had carried in a "grandfather bag" from Berlin to Singen, in a sheer unending supply that sustained us for the duration of the journey. I do not know anymore at what time on our trip I recognized the inestimable help Mrs. Meier was giving me. Her resolute spirit had supported mine. Indeed, she had proven her trustworthiness, because, throughout the trip, she had had only one goal: my safety. At the time, I had no inkling that this concern of hers would continue and be extended to others in need in the future.

When it was time to leave for the meeting, we returned to the center of town. According to the previously established rules, we had to say good-bye to each other before I met the guide. Both of us felt that it was a forced separation: I knew that she cared about what would happen to me, and I was sad to see her go. Now I had to face alone the border crossing and the dangers connected with it. It was early for the meeting. While I watched Mrs. Meier walking away toward the Bahnhof, I was approached by a young man: I did not seen him coming; nor did I understand his words, although I should have expected him. The suddenness of his approach took me by surprise. I took a few steps away from him and realized that Mrs. Meier was still in the distance. When I called out to her, she turned and walked toward me. I indicated the young man, still standing on the same spot, and together we walked up to him. He was, of course, the right young man, holding my picture in his hand. The surprise was on him, because he did not understand that being fifteen minutes early could have caused such a confusion and anxiety in me. Now that a new situation had been created by the presence of Mrs. Meier, he was a perfectly reasonable and did not insist that she leave. He agreed easily to Mrs. Meier's suggestion that she stay in Singen until the next day, Sunday afternoon, when he would report to her of my being safely across the border.

"Tomorrow morning," she said, "will see me in church, lighting a candle for your safe passage." That was her adieu to me.

We separated and walked off in different directions. The young man recovered his bicycle nearby, and while pushing it with me by his side, he explained to me that, according to my uncle's letter, he intended to take me to his friend's house in Gottmadingen: the safest and shortest way would be to walk cross-country through the woods. He would ride his bicycle ahead of me, and I was to follow him at a distance of about one hundred yards and should keep an equal distance diagonally away from him. He would make sure that we would not lose sight of each other. Soon we had the streets of Singen behind us and entered the wooded area he had spoken of. He took the lead on his bicycle, and I followed him as he had asked me to do. I had no trouble keeping up with him. We entered a beautiful forest, a large stand of high-stemmed silver beeches with the first green just coming out. I knew such woods from my childhood in Wolfenbüttel: the Lechlumer Wald had been the goal of our family's Sunday afternoon walks, and the Elm, another wooded ridge in the same environment, was the preferred place for the monthly school field-trips (*Schule-Wanderungen*). Both the Lechlumer Wald and the Elm were lovely beech forests. Here I was, just having embarked on an adventure that might become dangerous at any minute, admiring the beauty of nature around me, instead of centering my thoughts on what might lie ahead! Was it a heightened sense of excitement that made me notice the details in this situation more than I usually would, or had long forgotten impressions of my childhood come up to flood my memory with happiness? I was enjoying this walk through the woods and forgot about all the lurking dangers. In this way, we might have walked nearly one hour, when we reached Gottmadingen in the fading light. We had left the forest and had entered a small street with a row of houses on one side, an almost rural environment. The guide stopped and waited for me to come up to him: evidently, we had reached Mr. Höfler's house. He preceded me up the few steps, knocked and entered, and I followed. I was embarrassed about this silent method, like "thieves in the night," of going into a stranger's house, but also aware that we behaved "according to plan." Mr. and Mrs. Höfler were waiting

for us and, in their friendly way, made me forget my embarrassment of having arrived in such an "abbreviated" way. The
young man from Singen (whose name I never learned) who had
so expertly guided me took his leave, after having informed us
that he would be back on Sunday afternoon.

After he left, Mrs. Höfler invited me to sit down and take supper with them, which I gladly accepted. It was a cold supper, as
is the custom in Germany and Switzerland. (The big warm meal
is eaten at noontime, when the children come home from school
and most family members have a one-hour break.)

This was our first occasion to talk and become familiar with
each other. I learned that Mr. Höfler and his friend from Singen
worked in a factory, named Fahr, in Gottmadingen. During
peace times, the factory had produced heavy agricultural machinery, but since the outbreak of the war, it specialized in manufacturing parts for the armament industry. Both he and his
friend had special IDs that entitled them to move about with
fewer restrictions than others. I was also told that Mrs. Höfler
was from Switzerland and had retained her Swiss citizenship
when she married. Swiss law permitted women either to retain
their citizenship when they married a foreigner or to have dual
citizenship. She mentioned that she often used her passport for
visits "at home." Such local visits were frequent, "*der kleine
Grenzverkehr.*" Her remark was casual, but later it became evident that our plan of rescue was set in motion by one of Mrs.
Höfler's visits "at home" in Stein am Rhein. They informed me
that they had a four-year-old daughter who was asleep now and
whom I would meet in the morning. Finally, they explained with
some embarrassment that there was no room in their tiny house
for an extra couch for me to sleep on, and they could only offer
me one of their own twin beds—one part of their *Ehebett* for the
night. They were to sleep in the other together.

I was touched by this extraordinary offer and suddenly became aware of the deep emotions which must have motivated
them to save a person's life—my life. I was trying to find an
explanation for behavior that had surprised me: the next morning I gained a glimpse of it.

Sunday morning started out gray and drizzly: not a good
omen for taking a walk. The window of the living room gave a

Lotte and her brother
Helmut, c. 1929

Below, left: Lotte's father,
Louis Schloss, 1913. Right:
Johanna Schloss (née
Bildesheim) and Carl
Bildesheim, Lotte's mother
and uncle.

Wolfenbüttel Schloss (castle), where Lotte attended school.
Photo by Wolfgang Lange.

Lotte's family's house on Lessingstrasse, Wolfenbüttel

Steps to the garden at Kladow

The house at Kladow

Lotte (upper right) with her
brother Helmut, mother (lower
right), and grandmother,
Jeannette Bildesheim.
Wolfenbüttel.

Helmut at Kibbutz Givath
Brenner, 1937

Herbert Strauss, c. 1940

Lotte in the 1940s

This picture, taken by Jean Friedrich during the underground period in Berlin, was used by a guide at Singen, near the Swiss-German border, to identify Lotte and facilitate her escape.

Aunt Ilse Schöneberg

Uncle Ludwig Schöneberg

August Sapandowski

Jean Friedrich

Luise Meier (left) and Gertrud
Höfler (later Eisele), early 1950s.
Courtesy of Gertrud Eisele.

Josef Höfler

Dr. Ilse Kassel

Dr. Kassel with daughter, Edith

road, however. We all knew that the plan might be danger-
s. In case it was, Mr. Höfler suggested we say (if questioned)
t I had just joined them on their walk to buy eggs from a
mer in the next village.

When the young man from Singen returned, we were ready
start. At the last minute, Mrs. Höfler came up with a brown
w hat with a bunch of artificial flowers in front and put it on
head. It was hiding part of my face and my short hair. I was
dapt my appearance to rural customs: for a woman to wear
at to church or on a Sunday visit was the local tradition, and
cepted the hat without demur.

We were ready to set out, the two men taking the lead, as
med natural. Mrs. Höfler and I followed with the little girl in
middle; we were holding hands. There was nobody else
und, except our little group. We passed by a farmstead of
eral buildings, but nobody was outside. A little cat ran across
path, and I promised myself not to be superstitious ever
in. As the road descended, we approached the spot where
guards were stationed. There was no barrier across the road,
no guardhouse, but two uniformed guards were standing
he ditch by the roadside. We continued to walk in the same
er as before: the men approximately ten yards ahead of us.
they came close to the guards, they stopped and bent down
how them their special IDs. While the guards looked at their
ers, we walked on in the middle of the road, and when we
e in line with the guards, we called a loud ''Heil Hitler!'' and
t on walking. We listened intently: would they want us to
w our papers? No call came, and in that second we knew: we
passed the danger! We could not believe our luck. If our
avior would not have given us away, we would have shouted,
ped for joy, hugged each other. It had been an incredible,
e moment for all of us. As intended, the guards had taken
or what we pretended to be: a family on a Sunday afternoon
ng. Had fate protected me—us? Was it a lucky accident, or a
ect plan?

he men joined us again, and we walked on as before. We
hed the hollow before the village of Randegg: the road
ed around, and we were out of the sight of the guards. Ac-
ling to plan, I knew that the moment would come to leave

Above: Lotte's mother's portrait from Jewish identity card. Left ear was required to be shown. Right: Wolfenbüttel Synagogue (1893–1938). Lotte's family lived in the house next door.

Memorial plaque for the Jews of Wolfenbüttel. Herbert Strauss second from left; Lotte second from right.

Above: Lotte and Herbert, 1960s. Left: daughter Janie (Jane Helen Jones). Below: Janie with husband, Robert E. Jones.

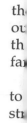

unencumbered view over fields, planted v
grain (as far as I could make out) and, in t
see a range of wooded hills. It would be tha
to traverse. The place by the window was
He stood there, almost like a statue, looki
through his binoculars. When I became cur
the fieldglasses and explained the situation t
that we would be able to walk through the
the way to Randegg, the border village at the
range. Randegg was the focal point we co
the path to the border would lead from ther
height and proceeded through the wood
formed by a *Wald Schneise*—forest aisle—cu
as though with a razor. He continued to e
forced by the bad weather to take the *chau*
road, connecting one village with the next. ?
the country created a pattern in the Germar
apple trees planted along them made them
and-buggy traveler from the distance (hor
were not so far away then). Mr. Höfler had
road because two border guards were perm
it. The plan for our walk now sounded com
see from the serious look on Mr. Höfler's f
ried. I reminded myself that my uncle's le
Mr. Höfler implicitly, which I was willing
the alternative dangers and could weigh
other.

Earlier that morning, Mrs. Höfler had be
fast and their little daughter. Now, howev
the table with the Bible open before her. H
over the big book; she was reading in a cor
became quite obvious to me then what the
help and face the resulting dangers.

I also met their daughter: she was a lively
behaved naturally toward me. I was glad
as her playmate for a while.

By noontime the fog had lifted, and the
too, so that the Sunday afternoon walk be
and acceptable prospect. Mr. Höfler stuck t

the country road. I was right: Mr. Höfler and his friend started to walk up a path on the hillside, leading toward the wooded stretch on top. They waited for us to join them.

I had made several attempts, earlier in the morning, to talk with Mr. Höfler about Herbert, but he had fended me off by saying, "Later, later, first you have to be safe before we think so far ahead." So I had to bide my time hoping that his remark was not only a pretext or even total avoidance of the subject. As we walked up the hill together, I realized that this was probably my only opportunity to bring up my request to help Herbert. I asked again: "Won't you help Herbert to cross, now that he has his ID from the Heeres- und Bewaffnungsamt Speer?" Their answer surprised me. They "would do what they could to help Herbert," but there was a condition attached to their help which I had to promise to fulfill first. I listened in astonishment as they explained to me that the border was like a sieve as far as the story of my crossing the border was concerned. A tale like this, if it became known, would be discussed on both sides of the border—was this the result of the *kleine Grenzverkehr?*—which might lead to their and their families' ruin and would make it impossible to help Herbert or anybody else across the border. I was surprised that the border, which had seemed hermetically closed to me, should be open to this kind of communication. I had vaguely anticipated that by assisting me they would be endangering themselves, if the border-crossing would go wrong, but I was shocked that they might face such consequences anyway. There was, of course, an obligation to prevent this from happening, which I felt very strongly. "I would tell a pack of lies" if that was necessary to protect them and wished advice from them on how to invent a story that would sound believable to the Swiss authorities.

Mr. Höfler was prepared for the question and suggested a "go-it-alone" story, namely, that I had known the area previously from hikes through the Hegau (west of Lake Constance), which is known for its beautiful walks. He told me the route, adding a few telltale markings along the way and also the name of a hotel, Hotel Lamm, in Gottmadingen, where I could have stayed overnight. It was vital to keep these details in my mind, because so much depended on them. I kept to that story until many years later when I had to "reverse" it to protect the Höflers by telling the truth. While we walked on the path uphill, we came to an understanding that each would do the best he could to help the other.

The hillside path had led us through meadows, but when we reached the top of the hill its character changed to a mere field path running alongside the edge of the wood. By this time, we had walked more than one hour, though I cannot be quite sure: the constant presence of danger and the accompanying tension might have altered my perception of time. I was also unaware until then of the astonishing achievement of the Höfler's four-year-old daughter, who had walked without complaining or showing any impatience or fatigue. This persistence in a four-year-old struck me suddenly as amazing. I also realized then that Mrs. Höfler's committing herself and the child to this dangerous rescue had been an act of unparalleled courage.

The first part, the Sunday afternoon walk, behind us, it was no longer necessary for Mrs. Höfler to accompany us, as we entered the forest. She and the child stayed behind to spare them the strenuous walk through the woods. I handed the hat back to her, tried to express my thanks—very inadequately—and said good-bye more with a smile than with words. We left them in a little thicket, sitting on a blanket that Mrs. Höfler had brought along. Any delay could be dangerous, and Mr. Höfler, during all this time, was on the alert: he knew from previous walks he had taken in anticipation of the Sunday "crossing" that the guards changed their positions frequently.

As we left Mrs. Höfler and her daughter behind, we entered deeper in the forest. It was a young beech forest, with densely grown underbrush. Mr. Höfler led us as we walked single-file through this rough terrain. He picked up a little branch from the ground and with his pocket knife started shredding it, so that they would be able to recognize the path they had to take on the way back. We walked through the woods not too far from its edge: light penetrated in shafts from the side, illuminating the landscape beyond the wood. While we walked, I tried to recapitulate the explanations I had been given about the special border situation. Every German schoolchild had learned that the Rhine River was the accepted German border, celebrated in patriotic poems and songs as *Vater Rhein*, "Father Rhine." It was not only the southern border between Germany and Switzerland, but also the western border between Germany and France. However, there were exceptions to this rule. The border we tried to reach was a Swiss enclave, reaching from the Rhine River northward in an oddly shaped zigzag line, having its history in a former principality, or a bishopric, whose traditions had been left in place since the Middle Ages. How exactly it had come about I do not know. In my uncle's letter to me in Berlin, and again in explanations from Mr. Höfler, I was made aware that I must be conscious of keeping to exact directions so that I did not stray accidentally back into German territory.

After we walked through the woods for approximately fifteen minutes, Mr. Höfler slowed down and then halted: we had arrived at the Swiss border. It was only a few meters from where we stood. As I knew, the border was a *Wald-Schneise*, a line cut straight through the forest as if drawn with a ruler. The aisle was about ten meters wide and looked like a logging-path. No fence or sign marked it as a border line. I doubt very much that I would have recognized it, even though I had been told what it would look like. Mr. Höfler pointed out the direction I had to take, once I had crossed the aisle: I could see the path—it lay straight ahead, once I had passed the *Schneise*. This, then, was the great step into freedom! Now that I had come so close, I was hesitating again. Old fears revived in me, and a new one was added. I was keenly aware that the step across the border might be the final separation from Herbert that I had anticipated with dread for weeks. The new anxiety was that I had become conscious of the many risks of this border crossing. For me, it had worked out by having been planned to perfection, but I was aware that many lucky accidents had accompanied my way from Berlin to this point. How could I trust fate to repeat these accidents? As I stood there, rooted, this moment seemed like a small eternity to me. I knew that this burst of confused feelings had to stay unresolved for now: I simply had to trust my luck—our luck—further. My two companions were indicating urgency: the danger in this situation must not be prolonged unnecessarily. I turned to them to say good-bye. At this short moment I could not find adequate words to express my gratitude and true feelings for what they had done for me. I hoped they knew how I felt. I ran down a small embankment, stood for a moment, and waved to them, as they turned to retrace the trail through the woods we had walked together. I was in Switzerland!

7

Our Helpers

AFTER WE HAD REACHED SWITZERLAND, we did not get in touch with Mr. Höfler or Mrs. Meier. They had sworn us to secrecy, because they feared that their rescue actions would become known and endanger them.

I never talked about Mrs. Meier or Mr. Höfler to anybody in Switzerland or in the United States. I did not know what had happened to them. The first sign of Mr. Höfler's fate I received in a peculiar way. The Consulate General of the German Bundesrepublik in New York City asked me to appear and testify under oath about Mr. Höfler's activities. It turned out that he had been arrested after one of his protégées aroused the attention of the police and gave away Mr. Höfler's name and activities during her interrogation. This happened in the spring of 1944, just one year after my safe passage. He was jailed in Konstanz: his imprisonment lasted eleven months, until, in April 1945, French troops conquered the area and liberated the prison. His life, at least, was saved, but he must have lost part of his belongings, because he had applied for indemnification for the injustices he had suffered under Nazi persecution for his humanitarian activities. It was the first time I had heard about his postwar life, and in my testimony at the consulate I did everything to help him. When I left the consulate, I was in a contradictory mood: I was saddened by the danger and losses Mr. Höfler had experienced but also felt a sense of relief that he had not suffered damages on my behalf, and even greater relief that he was able to take up a normal life with his family again. He was an unsung hero: he had helped twenty-eight persecuted Jews to cross illegally into Switzerland and be free.

I cannot be sure that my memory is correct but believe that this interview on behalf of Mr. Höfler took place in the late 1950s. From then on, I was troubled not to know anything about the fate of Mrs. Meier, since she and Mr. Höfler had been working together in their rescue action.

By the unlikeliest of chances I learned about her fate more than thirty years later—from an interview she had given to the London Wiener Library in November 1955, in connection with the Library's attempt to trace the fate of Jews and their helpers in Nazi Germany. When Herbert directed research on antisemitism in Berlin in the 1980s, four of his students worked on the same subject. One day, in the mid-'80s, they gave Herbert a transcript of Mrs. Luise Meier's deposition with the Wiener Library. It gave us the information on Mr. Höfler and traced the history of Mrs. Meier's persecution by the Nazis as well. She was arrested over the same incident that entrapped Mr. Höfler, and taken from Beleke/Westphalia to Singen where she was imprisoned. The Gestapo exerted considerable pressure on her to extort information about her anti-Nazi contacts. She relates that the "interrogations were very strict, but I was not beaten" and ascribes this to the fact that two of her sons had been killed in action and the third one was a prisoner of war. Her trial was delayed, because her case was transferred from one court to another, causing delays and gaining her time. As she described her eleven months in prison, she derived strength and faith from her daily prayers, although she was convinced that she would be sentenced to death for her "treasonous" activities.

In the spring of 1945, the prison was liberated by the French. While she was imprisoned, her apartment in Berlin had been looted and whatever property she had saved for Jews who had been deported had disappeared as well. She faced a postwar life of destitution and, as she reports in the interview, "she had difficulties in obtaining compensation from the government because she did not know who had looted her apartment in Berlin."

When I read her interview thirty years after it had been given—forty years after the fact—I felt great sorrow for her. Her helping others had completely disrupted her life and inflicted great material losses on her. She and the Höfler family lived by the precepts of their religion. I am eternally grateful to her for helping to save our lives.

8

Crossing the Border: Imprisoned and Interned in Switzerland, May 1, 1943–July 1943

CROSSING THE BORDER into Switzerland brought a strange sensation: looking up and down the *Schneise* and not seeing a soul. Between the crossing and thinking "my life has been saved!" was a matter of seconds. I easily found the path that would lead me toward the guide who was to take me deeper into Switzerland, so I could be sure not to be turned back. But only fifty yards ahead of me loomed an obstacle, or, at least, that was what I perceived it to be: a bench and three people sitting on it. Two young girls and a young man. At first, I was fearful that they might have seen me crossing the border. But then, as I approached them, I heard their lively voices, so I passed by with a friendly greeting in my non-existent Swiss German. I noticed that they were surprised to see me. They, too, had been on their Sunday afternoon walk, which had had a very different purpose from mine. As I continued on my path, I wished heartily that they would continue their pleasurable afternoon, undisturbed by my passing. I was determined to get to my guide before I was detected by anyone.

But it was not to be. The young man followed me and addressed me: "You have just crossed the border! May I help you?" As I looked at him hesitatingly, he continued, "You can trust me, I am Swiss." Denying that I had crossed the border or refusing his offer of help did not make sense and might appear unfriendly or even hostile. I could not find a pretext to refuse his company outright, and so it happened that we continued on the path together. Reluctantly I had come to the conclusion that it was no longer possible to meet the guide: he expected me to be alone and would not dare to contact me in the company of a stranger. There was a law in Switzerland that forbade guiding émigrés across the border (*Emigranten-Schlepperei*). It was illegal either to accompany a fugitive or even to give a fugitive directions to a border crossing. Getting caught meant heavy fines or even imprisonment for the guide, and the person attempting the crossing was turned back. (We became aware of such a case after the War, in which a friend of ours and her guide had been returned to Germany. Our friend was deported to Auschwitz. She survived by playing in the orchestra, but her guide perished in the Ravensbrück concentration camp.)

For many reasons, I could not mention to the young man that I expected to meet a guide, and was now afraid of looking for him. My chivalrous companion had no way of guessing my misgivings. Anyway, his well-meant protection was short-lived. A little further down the path, I had another "Swiss encounter." This time, it was the real thing: a Swiss border guard. He wore the gray military uniform of the Swiss army and carried a rifle across his shoulder. He was a very young man, reddish blond with freckles. He addressed me in much the same way as the young man had done, using almost the same words. His military appearance and attitude in the middle of a forest path amused me, but immediately thereafter I realized that showing my amusement would be counterproductive and probably a serious mistake: he might have the authority to refuse me entry or even to return me to Germany. That this face-to-face encounter came within the first five minutes after I stepped onto Swiss soil was daunting, and I remembered then that this was exactly the time to act on the instructions spelled out in my uncle's letter. In keeping with these rules, I found myself telling the Swiss soldier "that I would rather be shot on the spot than returned to Germany, where my Jewish family had perished." This speech of mine had an effect on the young soldier I had not anticipated. His face turned beet red, and his expression became horror-stricken. He shook his shoulders, as if to get rid of something unpleasant. Then he said in his slow Swiss-German dialect, "The Swiss do not shoot that fast!" He had his answer ready: he would take me to the customs house, the *Zollamt*, in Buch and "there we would see further." Without ado, that is what he set out to do. A nod and good-bye to the young man, and we were on our way, marching through the woods down the path into the valley, into the customs house in Buch.

There, in the *Zollamt*, I was received with a lot of curiosity and examined by a matron in a superficial way. The "cell" where I had to take off my outer garments had a mirror, and it revealed a secret: my hair was covered with little brown husks the beech leaves had shed as I walked through the underbrush. Thus, without knowing, I had given my secret away. The matron's search was mainly to find out if I was a smuggler of black market items. When she was satisfied that I was not smuggling anything but myself, her interest and the others' centered on questions of black market prices in Berlin. I could understand that these were realistic concerns of customs people, but they struck me as being almost unbelievable and incongruous compared to my own worries. No further questions were asked. They refused my request to telephone my uncle and aunt in Lausanne to inform them of my safe arrival in Switzerland. I knew that they would be worried because they knew the day of my arrival, almost to the exact hour. Their customs agents' argument was that they did not have the competence to authorize the call. I would have to wait until I was in the custody of the police of the next village, whom they had informed of my arrival.

This was a new experience for me: waiting to be taken into custody by a benevolent policeman! When he appeared, I found him a little grumpy: he had been disturbed on an "off-duty" Sunday afternoon, but appeared generally good-willed. He had come on his bicycle, which he was pushing now, with me on the other side. We were walking along a canal; it was a straight road and the policeman thought to fill the time by interrogating me about my way to and across the border. I had learned Mr. Höfler's lesson well, and it seemed that he accepted my story without questioning, though I was glad that I did not have to sit across a table from him to be scrutinized more closely.

In the summer of 1994, I learned from our files, deposited in the Schweizer Bundesarchiv, that he was the policeman in the village of Ramsen and that his name was Mr. Mösle.

The sky had cleared by the time we reached Ramsen in the late afternoon, and the sun was shining. We stopped before a two-story building that looked residential like all the others. Upon entering it, I found that it had more uses than I expected: besides being Mr. Mösle's residence, it was the police station and the jail for the village of Ramsen. Apparently, it was Mr. Mösle's intention to put me into a prison cell while he was wrote his report. I was a prisoner, and he acted according to Swiss law. By this point, I had developed a wait-and-see attitude, knowing that I could not interfere with what the Swiss authorities considered the lawful thing to do. It seemed ironic that the dangerous road I had chosen to escape should end with my imprisonment, though temporarily. Mr. Mösle opened the door to one of the cells and surveyed the room: it revealed, at least on the side I could see, walls and ceiling with peeling plaster, which had come off in large batches, and hay covering much of the floor. (In my mind, the cell was not even good enough for a drunken brawler!) But before I had time to pity myself, Mr. Mösle apparently came to the same conclusion. He closed the door and proceeded to the next room: it offered the same dismal picture. Mr. Mösle looked at the room and then turned toward me and gave me an appraising glance. His assessment of the situation was expressed in one short sentence: "I will introduce you to my wife; while am I writing the report you will stay with her." Human understanding had prevailed over rules and regulations. He then introduced me to his wife. She welcomed me with a smile, and I was happy to look upon a friendly face after this long and harassing day. She had just prepared "café complêt," the traditional Swiss Sunday supper, and she invited me to share it with her. We were soon chatting with each other as we sat in her comfortable country kitchen, and I tried to answer her questions about life in Germany as best I could.

I had only one wish, and as soon as Mr. Mösle appeared again, I asked him for the favor of telephoning my uncle and aunt in Lausanne. But again this request was denied, with the same pretext as before: "I have no authority!" It was his intention to take me to prison aboard the train that left Ramsen at 7:30 P.M. for Schaffhausen. We had to hurry, and so it was a fast good-bye and thanks to Mrs. Mösle. We made the train, and soon found a comfortable corner. A gentleman who had taken a seat in the open compartment across from us soon began a conversation with Mr. Mösle in a Swiss-German dialect I was not able to understand. I had the impression that the two men knew each other. I was glad to sit in my corner and be left alone to think my own thoughts.

Many years later I learned from my uncle that this stranger on the train was the intended Swiss guide. Although we had missed each other, he had made sure that I had arrived in Switzerland. How he had traced my steps since the time of my arrival to the 7:30 train to Schaffhausen, I never learned. He had not only followed me invisibly, but also sent a telegram to Lausanne: "Congratulations on your birthday," signed "Lotte." Had I have known of this telegram at the time it would have simplified my life considerably. In hindsight, the scene in the train is amusing: that this stranger—my guide—and the policeman were acquaintances and conducted a conversation even as they acted on opposing sides of the law.

That birthday telegram sent my uncle off to Bern the next day to the Eidgenössische Fremdenpolizei (Swiss Police Bureau for Aliens) with the request that I be released from prison and placed in his care. The answer he got was negative: "Your niece has to be in quarantine for three weeks."

When the train arrived in Schaffhausen, it was dark. Mr. Mösle and I walked from the station to the prison. I was not able to see much in the darkness but I realized that we were walking through the old center of Schaffhausen, where history goes back to the Middle Ages. I could make out some of the narrow stone façades of houses, unevenly jutting forward, forming little corners, and a lantern throwing a faint light on the cobblestones across the street. We entered a small square and there, in the back, were the police headquarters of Schaffhausen and its prison. Mr. Mösle took me inside. We entered a large room with desks that stood empty at this time. There were only two policemen around: they were on one side of the room and had guns in their hands. It was evident that they had been target shooting. The target on the other side of the room was riddled with holes. When we entered, they came forward to inquire our business. Mr. Mösle pointed at me and handed over his report. It was all very perfunctory, very few words were exchanged, and Mr.

Mösle, with a little nod to me, disappeared into the night to catch the train back to Ramsen.

One of the policemen took my name down, registered the exact time—it was 9 o'clock—took my watch into safekeeping, and told me that he would take me up to a cell in the women's prison. Electric light at this late hour was not permitted. I had to follow his flash light, so I walked behind him, following that little disk of light up several stairs until he stopped and opened a cell for me. We stepped into complete darkness and walked slowly until we reached an obstacle. It was a bed, he explained to me. I reached out, and my hand touched something prickly: a straw mattress and pillow and nothing else. The policeman, muttering something about tomorrow, withdrew. I was left in the darkness with two snoring voices and a feeling of loneliness settling on me. I lay down with my coat and shoes on and finally fell asleep. That was my first day in Switzerland.

Early the next morning, I was awakened by a metallic noise. The flap in the iron door was opened and *Frühstück*, breakfast, was pushed through: an aluminum container with lid and handle, containing milk-coffee, and a slice of bread.

Two other women were in the cell, but I could not exchange a word with them. They were Russian workers: the Germans had deported these workers in groups from Russia to Germany, where they had to do heavy agricultural work. These two women had had the luck to work in territory near the Swiss border, and when one of their group had escaped, they had followed. They had arrived only a few hours before I did.

Looking around, I saw that the cell contained four beds, a wooden table bolted down with benches at its sides, a corner with a washstand and a pail as toilet. We were on the attic floor: one of the walls had slanted windows through which we could see the windows of the connecting wing and those across from us, indicating that our cell was located on the inside of a courtyard. Sometimes, we could hear a voice giving an order, and men seemed to be marching or exercising. These details were not as interesting to me as they were to my Russian cellmates. At my request, the matron, a nice young woman, brought me a blanket, towel and soap, and some books to read. One of the books she gave me was a volume of short stories by Gottfried

Keller, the great Swiss writer. For the two girls she brought the Bible in the Russian language. From then on, they read the Bible to each other nonstop in loud voices. When their breath gave out, they climbed on their beds, standing on the metal-foot end and straining their necks to find out if they could see or hear anything of the Russian men in the courtyard who had crossed the border as they had. But it was an unsuccessful enterprise.

I cannot say that my own progress in getting acquainted with Gottfried Keller was any more successful. My concentration was lacking, and the whole reading exercise was more an attempt to hide my unhappiness from myself. The painful past threw its shadows and darkened every thought. I knew what had happened and what was still happening in Germany: I could not get away from it. I felt a dull ache, remembering it all. I think that the days in prison were the unhappiest I have ever lived through.

The first morning was interrupted by a doctor's visit. I had to step out into the corridor, and he examined me perfunctorily. He looked at my eyes and throat and made me lift my arms, after which he pronounced that I had to be in "quarantine" for three weeks and left. What had he meant? Was it isolation or three weeks more in prison? Either option was so oppressive that I shuddered to think of what lay ahead. Had I expected freedom too soon?

When I was returned to my cell, I found that the matron had left a questionnaire for me to fill out. For the next few hours I had to concentrate on answering it as conscientiously as I could. After all, Switzerland was a neutral country and had an embassy in Berlin, which might well make inquiries about my veracity. So, a long portion of the first day slipped by without my having had the opportunity to make the request to call Lausanne.

On the second day of my imprisonment, I was asked to appear for an interrogation. I was led to one of the offices, where a policeman was waiting for me to answer his questions. He was a serious-looking man, with long features and glasses askew, who looked at me suspiciously over their rim. The first part dealt with my border crossing, and again I repeated what Mr. Höfler had told me to say. The second part dealt with my life in Berlin before and while in hiding. I was hesitant because I did not want to jeopardize Herbert and all the people who had helped us.

Though the war had turned against the Nazis, had it turned decisively enough that the Nazis would not, or could not, plan to invade Switzerland? I told my interrogator that I would not answer a single one of his questions until he told me what would happen to these records if there were to be an invasion of Switzerland by Nazi Germany. He assured me in a most serious way that even in a war situation the documents would be safeguarded against falling into German hands.

Though I had my doubts about his answer, I saw no further way to escape from telling him what he wanted to know. At first, his questions were more general: about the food situation in Berlin, and whether I had been aware of any changes of mood. My answers to these questions had to be rather limited because of our special situation of having been in hiding. I told him about the few experiences and impressions I had had. Then he turned to personal questions. It was a very slow process because he insisted on directing one question at a time to me, then writing my answer down, and proceeding to the next. He asked me about my family's life and what had happened to my parents, about the night of escape and the months in hiding. He seemed to concentrate on these last months of underground life in Berlin down to the last detail. I was forced to mention names and addresses of people with whom I had been in contact. Though he had given me assurances of safety, I was still reluctant to tell him more than was absolutely necessary.

One of the names that crept up more frequently than others was Herbert's. To my bureaucratic policeman's consternation, I objected to having Herbert called my fiancé, because Herbert had not asked me to be his wife. During the entire interrogation I talked about Herbert as my "boyfriend," which was an accepted and honorable expression for a love-relationship between a young man and young woman in Berlin's "social order." But I soon learned that it was not so acceptable in Switzerland. Every time Herbert's name came up in my report, the policeman stopped and with a disapproving look asked me if I agreed to the word *Liebschaft*, which might be translated as "lover" or "lover-boy." I could hardly hide my amusement and gave my consent. At the end of three days of interrogation, when the policeman read the whole report to me for my signature, he still expected me to object to being placed so low on the totem pole of social order as to be associated with a "lover-boy." But I could not spare Herbert should he ever come to Schaffhausen prison from being *"die Liebschaft."*

On the fourth day of my prison stay a new "inmate" was added: a Swiss peasant woman, accused of having slaughtered a pig illegally and selling the meat on the black market. She was beside herself at being so accused and felt the shame of being jailed for such a minor incident. Having "ja nur ein Säuli g'schlacht!" was a natural event for her. She repeated this confession like a litany to me, hoping for understanding in her plight. She wiped the tears off her face, and I felt pity for her and tried to comfort her. At this time, I did not know how seriously the Swiss government was watching out for every infringement on the rationing system and especially for those undercutting this system, the black marketeers. The small state, in its landlocked isolation, had to be rather self-sufficient during wartime. At the beginning of the war, it had established the Wahlen Plan to make the smallest plot of land fertile. Black marketeers were punished severely. But, at the time of my imprisonment, I was not aware of these circumstances.

As the "Säuli" complaint went on and on, and the two Russian girls read the Bible to each other in stentorian voices, I wished myself far away from any "Säuli slaughter," from the girls, still reading the Bible to each other, and from my scandalized bureaucrat!

That wish was to be fulfilled sooner than I expected. My name was called out and I was informed that I had to be ready the next morning at five o'clock to be transferred. No explanation was given, and I considered quarantine and isolation with apprehension.

Early the next morning, I left the prison cell while Lydia and Natalie and the Swiss woman were still sleeping, and was introduced to Police Officer Mr. Brütsch-Mäder. He approached me with a friendly smile and told me that he was to accompany me on a trip to Lausanne: the train would pass through German territory—a German enclave—and German border guards might enter the train and would have the right to remove me. In order to avoid such a contingency, he would accompany me. He went on to explain, in ordinary sentences, not in police cryptics, that he would take me to a military refugee reception center, above Lausanne, called La Ramée, formerly a finishing school for girls. I was happy to hear this news: going to Lausanne meant that I could finally establish contact with my aunt and uncle.

From the beginning of our meeting, Mr. Brütsch-Mäder had tried to establish a friendly relationship between us. As the train began to move out of the Schaffhausen station, he started to draw me into a conversation, which was not difficult to do, because I was eager to have somebody to talk to. I was tired of being treated like a chess figure pushed silently from one place to another, not knowing what was happening.

I also found that Mr. Brütsch-Mäder was a good sightseeing guide. As the sun rose, sheets of white fog lifted and revealed that we were traveling through an undulating landscape of green meadows, with apple, pear, and cherry trees, some of them in bloom. They stood out like silhouettes on the green hills. The train stopped in Winterthur: the German enclave was behind us, but I had thought that Mr. Brütsch-Mäder had not worried overly much about it. He unpacked his breakfast and offered to share it with me, which I gladly accepted. I was very grateful for this gesture, because I did not believe that my "bureaucratic interrogator" would have been so generous. Accordingly, my confidence in Mr. Brütsch-Mäder grew. He did not ask me about my border crossing: I was glad not to have to tell him a lie. But then he became interested in knowing how I had spent the days in prison. Pondering the question, I realized that the desperation I had felt so keenly then was now tempered with a tinge of humor. I told him of the Russian girls and their Bible-reading in Russian and what consequences that might have for their future if they understood what they were reading. I also mentioned to him the Swiss peasant woman who, through tears, had told me that she had been imprisoned because she had slaughtered only "a Säuli." Her exasperation, expressed in Swiss-German dialect, had touched me because it contrasted incongruously with what I had gone through. The story made Mr. Brütsch-Mäder break into hearty laughter: "So, she confessed to you! It was for that purpose that I had put her into your cell!" I was crestfallen. Without realizing it, I had given her away. I told him how bad I felt, having been so used. But he did not listen: he was still in the whoops about his plan having worked out so well and imagining how this quasi-comedy scene had played out between us. Finally, he became serious again and readily promised to be lenient with her. I trusted his word but had to endure a sermon from him about the importance of the Swiss rationing system's not being undermined.

I also told him about the three-day-long inquiry about my life, especially my underground life of the last months in Berlin, and confided how the questioning policeman had degraded my "boyfriend" in Berlin to a mere *Liebschaft* in Switzerland. Both of us recognized the bureaucratic attitude behind his colleague's assumptions. Encouraged by his understanding, I went a step further in confessing to him that it was my intention to do everything in my power to bring the *Liebschaft* to Switzerland if I could find a way. Had I done right by telling him? I could not have been more surprised when he indicated that he might help to accomplish my plan: he himself had grown up in the border area of Schaffhausen and knew exactly where Herbert could cross the border unobserved. The only condition was that Herbert would have to dress like a day laborer. This was, of course, an obstacle, but I listened intently so that I could write it down later, in case the plan with Mr. Höfler would not work out. I was struck by the fact that here was a Swiss police officer who was ready to act against the law. Apparently, he did not believe in the outcry against more refugees, "Das Boot ist voll!"—the boat is full—which the Swiss had held as a shield against refugees wanting to enter their country. Or was the explanation that his rules and his sympathies were in conflict? I did not ask him any questions and took his assistance for what it was: a wonderful offer of help.

By now, the train ride had lasted almost three hours: it had stopped in Zürich, Fribourg, and Bern. I had seen a stretch of the Jura Mountains and had glimpsed some lakes—like blue glaze blinking from the distance—fields and meadows rising toward woods and rocky mountain sides. This Switzerland *was* a beautiful country. When we were not far from our destination, Mr. Brütsch-Mäder prepared me for "a spectacular view" that would come up on our left side. I sat obediently to watch for it.

Terraced vineyards glided by the train, descending at high speed, when suddenly the view over the entire expanse of Lake Geneva stretched out before us with all its blue hues and sparkle in the sun. On the other side of the lake, the sweep of this scenery came to rest on the chain of the French Alps, with its mountain sides and peaks covered with snow. It was breathtaking: nature had created an excess of beauty. The sky formed a shimmering dome over the exhilarating scene; it had an air of freedom which I always connected with this landscape and I extended this perception, over many years, to all of Switzerland. Whenever I come to Switzerland, be it by plane, by car, or by train, I look up to the sky and am conscious of the liberating breath of freedom I experienced then and can still feel now. As the train sped through the vineyards and little wine villages, my eyes tried to register all the different spots of beauty and did not know where to look until the train was at the lakeside and rolled into the station in Lausanne a few minutes later.

Mr. Brütsch-Mäder had given me permission to call my aunt and uncle and lent me the money to do it. From a telephone booth in the station I dialed their number. When Ilse heard my voice, she gave a shriek of surprise and then a torrent of words followed. My aunt—Ilse, as I called her from then on—tried to tell me several things at the same time. She was so happily excited that it was too confusing for me to grapple with the onslaught of information, and because whatever I could do was dependent on Mr. Brütsch-Mäder, I handed him the receiver to let him decide what to do next. He listened and then accepted the invitation to their home, with the condition that he had to deliver me at Camp La Ramée before noon. That gave us almost two hours' time. When our taxi arrived at the Avenue de Rumine, Ilse was expecting us. It was a joyous reunion for both of us. More than that, she looked at me like the lost and restored daughter of the family: she had helped to save my life. I hugged her with all my heart!

Then Ilse led us up to the first floor: we entered a large, beautiful apartment, elegantly appointed, with modern and post-Impressionist paintings giving it a special style. She invited us to the dining room, where the table had been laid for an elaborate breakfast. That sight alone made me think of earlier times, times long since past. I was also glad that my family was reciprocating Mr. Brütsch-Mäder's offer to share his breakfast on the train: no doubt we both enjoyed this reception.

Ilse was an easy conversationalist, and soon she and Mr. Brütsch-Mäder were in a lively conversation, while I had only one wish: a bath. It was such a joy to soak and splash in the warm water and wash all the prison dirt off! Soon, though, there was a knock on the door: Uncle Ludwig had come back from the golf course and wanted to see me urgently. I wrapped myself in a big bath towel and opened the door for him. I never had seen Ludwig with an expression like this: his face was shining, and he had a fierce light in his eyes as he hugged me with both arms, saying "Du bist die Einzige, die wir gerettet haben," and he repeated, "The only one, the only one!" I felt then that his action to get me out of Germany had preoccupied him so totally that he could not think of anything else, but, in hindsight, his remark might have been a confession of not having been involved seriously enough before in getting his family out and an indication of his guilt feelings. From then on, Ludwig stayed involved in the fight against Nazi Germany in any way he could. He had secret access to the German embassy in Bern. His former chauffeur in Berlin, Jankowiak, whom we called Janko, was now an employee at the embassy as a diplomatic courier. They had stayed in contact with each other, and whatever Janko could find out about the contents of the secret messages he had to transmit, or about transports of gold from Germany to the embassy, was then communicated to Ludwig and transferred by Ludwig to Swiss military counterintelligence. This activity became one of his main obsessions during the later war years. Janko's application to this task and total dedication to the cause of espionage against Nazi Germany came about when his son, a student at the University of Munich, had been caught in the circle of Professor Huber and Hans and Sophie Scholl, two of his students. They were arrested when they floated antigovernment leaflets from a university balcony and were subsequently tried and executed by the Nazis.

Ilse, too, was very much involved in all Ludwig's plans and activities: she was to type the correspondence as well as many of these secret plans. But in her own right she was the engaged and open-hearted person who befriended everyone who had to lead "a poor emigrant's life" in Lausanne. Many of these immigrants had come to Switzerland from Austria, at the time of the Anschluss in 1938. The people of this group were called *Emigranten* and did not have to stay in camps but did not receive work-permits. They were "maintained" by the Jewish Emigrant Aid Society, but that was barely enough to scrape by. So Ilse did her best to help with her own means and also involved her church, the Lutheran Reformed Church, in assisting Jewish refugees. Jews living in Switzerland, insignificant in number, played a minimal role in Swiss society. Christian churches, including small religious sects, generally aided only their own church members. I know of one church group, in particular, headed by a Mrs. Kurz, who had worked with a handful of Protestant pastors to have more Jewish refugees admitted to Switzerland. She did what lobbyists do nowadays, but at that time was unheard of: she went to the Swiss parliament and buttonholed any parliament member or official and told him that "This condition can no longer go on: it kills me!" In Swiss-German dialect: *"Mi sprengt's fast!"* She gave Sunday sermons on this theme, and finally she created an atmosphere in which the politicians had to listen. It was a moral victory for the Christian churches in Switzerland: their attitude was very different from the German Christian churches, where wrongheaded patriotism led them to follow Hitler.

Ludwig had left Berlin at the end of 1936. It was after the Olympiad in 1936, when the official acquiescence toward foreigners and Jews had abruptly deteriorated. For Ludwig the end had come early one morning when he was to take his daily swimming exercise and had been confronted with a sign: "Juden ist der Aufenthalt verboten!"—Jews are not allowed. That was the final push for him to leave Germany. He prepared for a long trip to Argentina to visit his brother who had just settled in Buenos Aires, and to see a boyhood friend from Salzkotten who had become a Catholic missionary in the South American wilds to convert and care for a South Brazilian tribe. The fate and the mission of "Pater Toelle" had long exercised my uncle's imagination: he had endowed this life of sacrifice with a "Dr. Schweitzer" romanticism, because his work in Lambaréné had created admiration and attention around the world. But plans for a visit had to be scrapped: an expeditionary force would have been necessary to reach Pater Toelle at his mission, so Ludwig had to be content with seeing his friend in Europe whenever he was there for a longer home visit. But Ludwig's stay in Buenos Aires resulted in his obtaining Argentine citizenship in a short time with the help of his brother and sister-in-law who spoke Spanish and Portuguese.

When he returned to Berlin in 1937 as an Argentine citizen, a neutral alien, some conditions in his property status had changed. Nevertheless, he did not want to stay in Germany. It was then that he arranged for an "Aryan takeover" of his business by Miss Henriette Schneider. Shortly thereafter, both Ludwig and Ilse left Berlin. It was not an official emigration: they went on a one-year cruise around the world on an English ship, with the secret intention not to return to Germany but to wait out the end of the Third Reich in Switzerland.

They settled in Lausanne, when Ludwig was fifty-five years old and Ilse thirty-one. They thought they would wait until the German nightmare would disappear, and they could return to Germany and continue their lives there, he the enterprising and successful businessman, she the artist-wife.

Ilse had been a student at the Berlin Akademie der Künste and had been admitted to the master class of Emil Orlik. Her career was cut off just when it might have taken off. In Lausanne, she had set up a makeshift studio in their apartment, but Ludwig did not have much sympathy for her art. He did not tolerate lightly that she failed to devote herself completely to him. He was no doubt a demanding and authoritarian husband. Money, too, might have played a role: during the war, borders were closed and currency transfer restricted. It would have been difficult and costly to pay for gallery space to exhibit her paintings. Years after the war, Ilse turned to professional painting with renewed intensity and became quite successful in her field. She painted some portraits and flower arrangements, then her interest turned to dance, specifically to ballet. Her preoccupation with modern dance may have had its origin in a friendship with a young Lausanne woman, Diane, who was a professional dancer and Ilse's model while they lived in Lausanne. From her,

Ilse learned the basic steps and movements of modern dance, and this enabled her to draw ballet scenes during performances. In seconds she caught the gist of a scene and brought it to paper, later to transpose it on copper plates. Her most spontaneous work was created in this way.

My uncle, too, was restricted in his activities in Lausanne. He must have realized soon that to wait out the end of the war in Switzerland had been a wrong decision: Swiss law forbade "tolerated" foreign residents from engaging in any and all business activity. His inactivity was an irritant to him. He, who had always thought of new ways of enlarging business and had basked in the admiration of his many employees who had seen in him the pinnacle of success, was reduced to the isolation of a prematurely retired person.

After the war, he found that he could never recover the past. He was one of the first businessmen to return to Berlin after the war to rebuild his former business in the Leipzigerstrasse: the building had been damaged by a bomb. However, conditions in Berlin changed, at first imperceptibly, then with giant steps. After the war Leipzigerstrasse was located in East Berlin, which became the so-called Soviet-Occupied Zone. German Communists who had fled from the Nazis to Russia were sent back from Moscow to take over the East German government in East Berlin. Walter Ulbricht became the first East German dictator. West Berlin was a free enclave within the Communist Zone, which became the East German State, called the Deutsche Demokratische Republik (DDR), though it had nothing democratic in it left.

Understandably, this development was a terrible disappointment to Ludwig and his planning for the future. He kept the small branch store at the Kurfürstendamm, located in a well-known movie house, named Marmorhaus under the regime of Miss Henriette Schneider. Ludwig infrequently went to Berlin and during these visits he lived in Kladow. But his true home was now Lausanne, and he was always glad to return there. Ilse, too, had lost interest in Berlin: her parents had gone back to Wittenberg when Berlin was severely bombed and had died there of typhoid fever.

In 1963, after the Communists built the Wall between East and West Berlin, Ludwig sold Kladow and the house he still owned in the West End, and closed the branch store on the Kurfürsten-damm. We met him at that occasion: it was his last visit to Berlin. He died in Lausanne in 1968.

When Herbert was the director of the Zentrum für Antisemi-tismusforschung (Center for Antisemitism Research) at the Tech-nische Universität in Berlin from 1982 until 1990, we often asked Ilse to visit us. At first, she postponed it from year to year, until it became quite clear that she "did not want to see Berlin again."

Every Jew—and often non-Jews as well—who experienced Nazism, directly or indirectly, suffered from being caught in the Nazis' spider web: being in the center meant extermination, and at its rim meant stunted education, development, and growth and often the onset of guilt feelings that grew with time and distance.

But, on that day when I arrived in Lausanne, May 7, 1943, this later insight was still hidden from us, and we were happy, even exulted together, because I had escaped.

When I entered the dining room again, there had been a com-plete change of scenery. The breakfast things had been removed and now large maps covered the surface of the table. In the living room I heard the staccato of the typewriter. My uncle and Mr. Brütsch-Mäder were bending over the maps, and Mr. Brütsch-Mäder was dictating the minute details of an escape route for Herbert. That they had taken on Herbert's escape as an issue of their own was wonderfully reassuring to me. For the first time, I felt—as Mr. Friedrich and Herbert had tried to im-press on me earlier—that my own escape might open the possi-bility for Herbert to follow.

The irony of fate took over, six weeks later, when Herbert was imprisoned in Schaffhausen after he had crossed the border. He, too, had to go through three days of interrogation, and he, too, had to deny that he had been shown the way, or had any helper. For three days, he sat across the same desk answering questions, unaware that his interrogator knew everything about him, be-cause this man across the desk was none other than Mr. Brütsch-Mäder, the policeman I had confided in. He knew that *die Lieb-schaft* had arrived!

My brief time with my family was nearing its end fast. Mr. Brütsch-Mäder had orders to take me to Camp La Ramée by noontime. Being with Ilse and Ludwig was like an emotional homecoming, but we knew that we would see each other soon again, because the camp was not far from them, only a short taxi ride up the hill. Camp La Ramée was a large building on a green hillside, overlooking town and lake below with its beautiful mountains as backdrop. But there was no time to admire the view because formalities took over. Mr. Brütsch-Mäder handed my police records to the camp director and exhibited a formality he had not shown earlier. I understood. I was sorry to see him go without being able to thank him. I knew that behind the harsh façade I had experienced in prison, you could find understanding and human impulses to help if you were lucky as I was.

Throughout my time in Switzerland, I ran into more of these contradictions, which led to the feeling that much of the official attitude had to do with the exclusionary character the Swiss government wanted to show to this wave of emigration. What was really happening in Germany had been published in Swiss newspapers as early as 1942 and 1943; but many of the Swiss did not fully grasp the enormity of the events. They understood their mistake too late. For many of them the end of the war precipitated a time of soul-searching and reassessment.

When the war drew to a close and the defeat of Germany was imminent, the Cantons and the Federal Police Department in Bern mounted an energetic drive to remind us refugees that we were not welcome to stay. Herbert and I had never planned to stay and early on had been in touch with friends outside the country about our emigration decision. Quite a few friends in Switzerland wanted us to stay and build on Herbert's successful study at the University of Bern and on the esteem his professors had expressed for him. Herbert had completed a *summa cum laude* Ph.D. thesis and his doctoral examination within the short period of three years. Many of our acquaintances believed that he would be useful to the country's education. Some academics urged the University to make a place for him, but the positions available were not only scarce but also promised to longtime assistants. Serving for years as an editor of his professor's several publications, without the promise of an independent position, was too insecure a proposition to build on. Our friends' initiative was well meant, but Herbert thought that it would not be realistic because teaching history, even modern European history, was the prerogative of the natives and bureaucratic elites: an outsider would not fit in.

Our choices as to where we would ultimately settle down were as yet quite open, but in 1945 we started to discuss these choices. One idea was that we would return to Berlin and that Herbert would help rebuild Jewish communal life, but this idea did not stand up well alongside our feelings about Germany. The idea of going to Palestine also held great attraction for us but was discarded after a long period of consideration, because during Herbert's university years, it had become clear that his future was to pursue an academic career, for which Palestine did not offer the right conditions at that point in its history. Encouragement from his professors and our friends, however, reinforced the idea that a university career should be his life's goal, in which I fully concurred.

Settling in the United States emerged as the best possibility. A Berlin friend of Herbert's, who had emigrated to the United States and after the war served in the United Nations Relief and Rehabilitation Agency organization in Europe, and later as an interpreter with the American team at the Nuremberg war crimes trials, visited us in Switzerland and offered enough help and information for us to plan seriously. We had numerous talks about nationalism and, without question, were strongly attracted to life in a democratic state like the United States. The United States would be neither a temporary asylum that barely tolerated us nor an exile that would exclude us from living in the Jewish community and sharing fully as equals in the life of the country.

However, despite the fact that we were loosely controlled by the police, Switzerland not only had saved our lives but also had given us many happy moments. After the war we often went to Bern for visits with our friends and spent our vacations in the Swiss mountains.

This leads me back to where I jumped my chronology, to our Swiss story: Camp La Ramée had been a girls' boarding school (*Mädchen Pensionat*), but during the war it had been converted to an *Auffanglager* or reception center where all refugees had to be accommodated until the further needs or wishes of host country and/or émigré could be determined.

The building was large and friendly looking and had a sizable garden. I was assigned a bed with a little night table, a closet space—with nothing to put in it as yet—and in a separate corner were sinks with running water. All the rooms were well equipped and airy, and most of them had a sweeping view over the lake. These were almost luxurious surroundings compared to the prison in Schaffhausen I had left early that morning. We were four to one room. Meeting my roommates presented some difficulties because none of them spoke German. I did not know then that communication with them would present a much deeper problem than I had anticipated: one was a Russian woman with ardent Communist convictions that she was hardly able to express. She was able to show her hostility in many ways, however. There was also the "light-hearted" girl from Paris— that was the way I described her in a letter to Herbert written at the time, using her own ironies. She, like many others, had emigrated from Poland or Yugoslavia to France either before or during the Blitzkrieg and was caught in France during the on- slaught of the German armies in May 1940. To avoid being caught by the conquering Nazis, they had fled to southern France and Vichy France where they had lived a precarious life, avoiding open persecution while feeling the hidden threat of an imminent takeover of Vichy France by Hitler's Germany. A friend, Yvette Wertheimer, whom I met later, who had lived first in Paris and then in Vichy France from 1940 to 1943, with an ironic smile described the situation during these years with a simple "on se débrouille" (one manages). When the Allies landed in North Africa, the long anticipated fear turned into re- ality as the German army moved into unoccupied southern France, and this time the French police did the bidding of Hit- ler's Germany, to their undying shame. The police came to the refugees' houses and delivered them to collection points, where they were transported to the extermination camps in Poland. For many, it was the second time they had to flee for their lives in a short time. How they managed it and somehow kept their equi- librium I do not know, because they, too, must have lost mem- bers of their families to Nazi persecution, and it seemed probable that they themselves had lived in misery during the last years without the means to provide for themselves. Crossing the mountains into Switzerland must have been for many of them a very hazardous adventure.

I expected that the extreme situations we all had experienced would create a common bond between us, but that was not the case. Incredibly, I learned immediately that there was a schism between us that could not be bridged, then or later. Was the seed for this hostility laid in the nineteenth century when Polish Jews emigrated en masse to the United States? When they had traveled through Germany, had they felt that they were not respected by German Jews? Or was their hatred more recent? I thought that perhaps our experiences might exert a pressure that would unify us into the belief in a common Jewish fate. But to them I was not Jewish: I was *deutsch*, which was meant as a curse word and was not even good enough for me. The superlative for *deutsch* was the French word *boche*, which they used to indicate that I had possibly conspiratorial connections to Nazi Germany! I could not account for their attitude, or, yes, for their ignorance. I became aware that by talking to them, I would not be able to right the injustice they were doing to me: it would create only an untenable situation of loud but ineffective scenes between us. I was terribly hurt, but kept my equanimity, though with an effort, in order to keep the peace, even if it created a barrier between us.

My loneliness at the camp did not last long. Among other people there, I met two couples, both elderly, who befriended me. One was of Austrian and the other of Russian background: Dr. and Mrs. Kroner and Mr. and Mrs. Freundlich. I have a clear memory of them for very different reasons. Dr. Kroner was a good pianist and accompanist and contributed much to the camp's music life. We enjoyed the variety of classical and lighter music he was able to offer us. My contact with the Freundlichs, especially with Nina, was different. On their long odyssey of escapes through Nazi-occupied territory, they had lost their son to deportation, a tragedy that surrounded her with a lasting sadness. I liked and pitied her and did what I could to comfort her. Our friendship lasted for many years.

Camp La Ramée had a civilian director: it was his task to deal with us, the refugees, according to the rules established by the military. All these reception centers were administered by the Swiss military, and as a result, La Ramée had a complement of soldiers who worked under the authority of the *fourier*, a sergeant or quartermaster. He was the unquestioned authority in the camp, because he had to deal with the organization of the provisions, when the distribution of scarce food in wartime Switzerland had created a special problem. Accordingly, the portions in La Ramée were small, but with the "material" help of Ilse, I could help myself and others too.

During wartime and in peacetime, the Swiss army had the "draft" or universal military conscription: every Swiss young man had to serve two or three years in the army. He was called a "recruit," and after his initial time of service was regularly called up for reserve duty, depending on his military rank. I also learned that their will to defend themselves was a traditional attitude, shared by almost everybody—at least during these wartime years. Whenever one entered a Swiss household where husband or sons were home, one could observe the well-cleaned military uniform on a hanger on the door knob and the rifle standing at the ready beside it. At first, such a scene took me by surprise, but I soon understood that Swiss patriotism was very different from German nationalism: they did not want to conquer but to defend their country and to be free men.

Camp La Ramée was full of young recruits busy with their different chores, which did not leave the refugees much to do. Most of the refugees' time was a game of waiting until the war ended. The hope was to find and rejoin their families and start a new life somewhere, or to "go home."

Meanwhile, we tried to keep ourselves busy with the few tasks we were allowed to do. We did kitchen or dining room service, or we talked and did stitchery which went together very well and served a practical purpose: upgrading the small wardrobes almost everybody possessed. On some evenings the dining room was changed into an auditorium where recitations and readings took place, or a concert was given. There was an upright piano, and Dr. Kroner was the accompanist for any volunteer with a good, or not so good, voice. I remember two evenings of recitals of Schubert songs: to the music and words of Goethe's "Über allen Wipfeln ist Ruh" one succumbs to one's emotions without reservations.

I soon discovered that recruits had other tasks to perform besides doing chores in the camp. On the day of my arrival in the camp, I applied to the director for permission to visit my uncle and aunt, but he refused. It was against the rules to grant a visit during the first week of a stay, and, in addition, the camp was in a four-week quarantine. (What the affliction was he did not say.) I was upset by this denial of a visit to my family, which seemed incomprehensible in my situation. On the day of my arrival in Lausanne, we did not have the time for personal conversation. My need to talk with my uncle was pressing, a compulsion to tell him what had happened in Germany, as if through the telling part of the burden of what happened to my parents and me would be lifted from me. I could not bear to be the sole survivor and somehow hoped that Ludwig, who had been so emotionally bound up in extricating me, could also extricate my parents from Poland and Herbert from Germany.

I was denied permission to visit them, but Ludwig intervened and was successful. Within a few days I was allowed to visit. However, I had to be accompanied by a recruit. So, one afternoon I left in the company of a soldier in uniform, a rifle slung over his shoulder: I walked ahead, he a short distance behind me. Our destination was the Avenue de Rumine, but I do not know anymore how we reached it or how many faces turned after us. When we arrived, we were received cordially, and the young soldier—eighteen or nineteen years old—was ushered into the kitchen to have s'vieri (coffee and cake) with Angèle, the maid. The rifle lay on the kitchen table, while the two of them had a lively conversation.

I felt happy in Ilse's and Ludwig's company that afternoon. To owe somebody your life creates a bond all of its own and carries with it not only an obligation of gratitude but also the wish to give trust and affection in return.

The lasting memory of that afternoon was my walk with Ludwig. As we went up to the Mon Répos Park and farther up the hillside, I explained to Ludwig how the hatred for the Jews had been widened by Hitler and his hangmen step by conscious step since 1938, until it had created a wall of separateness that isolated the Jews from civil society. I told him how this persecution of the Jews had become the center of Nazism. I talked to him about my parents and my inability to save them, about the disappearance of friends, about the way Jewish life had been extinguished like candles blown out by a whiff of ill wind, and that I would never be able to forget what had happened.

As I became adjusted to camp life, I did not anticipate that anything in my life would change soon.

An encounter during my second week in La Ramée proved this assumption wrong: somebody tapped me on the shoulder, and as I turned around, I saw an elderly gentleman who launched excitedly into the story of his and his wife's escape from Germany a few days before. I stood rooted, listening to Mr. Schindler's story: "We lived in Berlin and had no prospect of emigrating. We had known Mrs. Meier through a relative of ours and asked her for help when our deportation became imminent. She reacted immediately and in a short time found a hiding place for us in a small Westphalian town that she knew well. But everything went wrong the moment we entrusted our host, a hotel owner, with our true identities, and we were asked to leave. We were desperate and phoned Mrs. Meier in Berlin for advice. After a short interval she instructed us to travel to Singen on a prearranged day and wait at a certain time and place to be contacted. We acted as she had told us: in Singen we were met by a young man who took us to a hiding place in the nearby forest, where he told us to wait. By nightfall, he returned and led us through woods and meadows onto a path close to the Swiss border. He indicated the exact direction we were to follow, and within a short time my wife and I had reached the border safely." He then added, as an afterthought, that he was to give me regards from Mr. Höfler. I was stunned into silence. While listening to Mr. Schindler's story, I underwent a range of emotions, ending in exhilaration, when I became aware that the unbelievable had happened! Mrs. Meier and Mr. Höfler had acted together in this rescue effort, only a few days after I had left. My mind raced! Within seconds, what I had dared not hope flooded my feelings: they will bring Herbert safely across the border, too! Even when my old fears came back, Mr. Schindler's story had brought this hoped-for future a giant step closer.

I was also glad to learn from this story that the Sunday afternoon walk escape route had been abandoned as too dangerous. The new route by night, through the woods and meadows seemed safer, at least as Mr. Schindler described it to me. (A few weeks later that luck changed, when sixty English prisoners of war attempted a break from their German POW camp, and the only route to freedom led to Switzerland. From that time on, roads along the border were patrolled by armed border guards on bicycle, accompanied by trained shepherd dogs. Luckily, I did not know about these changes until Herbert was safely across.)

My anticipation of a happy future further escalated when I was approached by another newcomer to the camp a week later, a nice-looking woman in her fifties, Mrs. Wally Heinemann. She, too, had greetings from Mrs. Meier and Mr. Höfler for me, but, most important, she brought direct news from Herbert— wonderful news! I learned that, after my crossing, Mrs. Meier and Mr. Höfler had met and had lost no time in setting up rescue plans.

As she told me the story of her escape, I realized how strangely interwoven it was with my own: they both were played out in the same time-frame, early spring 1943, when she was in hiding with Mrs. Meier in Berlin-Grunewald, and my uncle, in Lausanne, was setting up the details of my escape.

A few weeks earlier, while I was still in Berlin, two of Mrs. Meier's friends, Mrs. Kurt and Mrs. Franken, had made the attempt to escape to Switzerland. Mrs. Meier had expected to hear of their success and was hoping that her friend Mrs. Heinemann could take the same route as they had. After their safe arrival in Switzerland, her two friends, Mrs. Kurt and Mrs. Franken, contacted my uncle in Lausanne. That they turned to him was a lucky coincidence: Mrs. Franken had been my uncle's secretary in Berlin. They asked him for help in returning their identification papers to Mrs. Meier in Berlin, so that others might be able to use them. He agreed to do what he could, and a short time later Jean Friedrich turned up in Mrs. Meier's apartment in Berlin and handed her the two identification papers.

This visit was probably a pivotal point in both Mrs. Heinemann's and my escape stories. Mr. Friedrich told Mrs. Meier of nearly completed arrangements for my escape, and then suggested that she accompany me to the border. Mrs. Meier readily agreed to this suggestion. Her company during the railroad trip had added greatly to my feeling of security, but it was her presence in Singen that started a sequence of events, as if a wheel had been set in motion.

Having met my guide in Singen, Mrs. Meier told me at our good-bye that she would await the report of my safe crossing the next day and light a candle for me at Sunday Mass in church. On the Sunday afternoon after my crossing, Mr. Höfler had informed Mrs. Meier of my safe escape: this way, two kindred spirits had met. Both of them were guided by the same motives and encouraged by having snatched an intended victim from the Nazi terror. At that very moment, they set up a rescue-operation: Mrs. Meier in Berlin, Mr. Höfler in Singen/Gottmadingen. They created an escape system, something akin to the underground railroad in the United States during slavery and Civil War times, when slaves were handed from place to place to gain their freedom.

Mr. Höfler came to Berlin to set up details for Mrs. Heinemann's escape, as well as Herbert and Lutz's. As she had helped me, Mrs. Meier now assisted Mrs. Heinemann to Singen, and from there Mr. Höfler took over, guiding her through the woods by night "bis sie drüben war" (until she was on the other side). When Mrs. Heinemann contacted me in Camp La Ramée and related the story to me, less than three weeks—five prison days included—had elapsed since my own escape.

In simple, everyday language, she told me that the date for Herbert's and Lutz's border crossing was set for June 13 (1943), but the news had an extraordinary effect on me. I could barely contain the happiness that flooded me. June 13, 1943 was the day of Whitsuntide, or *Pfingsten* in German. (The weekend of *Pfingsten* is a general holiday, frequently used for family outings *in die Natur* [into nature], which, at that time of rejuvenated green, held many attractions. During my childhood, our family too, followed this tradition: we mostly went to the Harz Mountains to walk in the Tannenwälder [fir woods unique to this landscape]).

I knew that the date of June 13 was carefully chosen for its

Volksfest character: many soldiers would be on furlough, and controls in the overcrowded trains would be eased. I could hardly believe that only three weeks separated Herbert and me: twenty-one days I wished would be fleet as the wind. Herbert would be safe! Our future together could not come fast enough.

Many unhappy hours came to my mind, when I had to leave Berlin without him, and the teary scene of our good-bye at the Anhalter Bahnhof, when I thought, "I never will see him again." I must have smiled to myself as I recalled how, by an ironic twist of fate, Mrs. Meier had met Mr. Höfler, an encounter that Mr. Höfler had wanted to avoid, to protect his anonymity. I remembered when, shortly after Mrs. Meier and I separated in Singen and Mr. Höfler's assistant approached me before the appointed time and I was so startled, that I called out to Mrs. Meier to return. My moment of fear and confusion in Singen had created a *fait accompli*: four people had already been saved, Herbert and Lutz would follow soon, if our luck held out!

It is impossible to ignore the many lucky breaks we had had since our first escape, and how they all interacted in a crucial way to save our lives. Of course, there was a well-thought-out plan behind our moves, but it was and still is—and will always be—hard to believe that we got through this maze of terror unscathed. Why we had been singled out for survival and millions of innocent victims had to die, I will be forever unable to explain. I have come to the conclusion that it was luck, an accident, that we were able to continue on into a full and active life with each other, our friends, and our family. We stayed involved in our communities all our lives.

The night of June 13 was a radiant night: moonlight flooded the landscape. Ribbons of light made the lake sparkle, and the snowcapped mountains in the distance glowed in the night sky. The pines in the garden of La Ramée stood glistening, as did every tree, bush, and fence—all throwing deep shadows on the ground. As I stood at the open window of La Ramée, this beauty did not make me cheerful, as it had done so often before. On the contrary, it scared me. This was the night of Herbert's and Lutz's crossing: I was aware that the brightness of the night posed a definite threat to them. Didn't they have to traverse flat meadows and a possibly dangerous road? Couldn't their every movement give them away?

With all these thoughts in my mind, I was standing motionless at my observation post when I noticed that a cloud bank sailed across the sky, concealing moon and landscape for minutes. It was a short interlude, then the sparkling night returned. But from then on new clouds floated by, darkening the sky for short periods. This alternating sky—rushing clouds with moonlit intervals—kept me in strong suspense. I wished that I had a magic spell to hold the clouds in place, just as on the night of our escape from the Gestapo I had wished to arrest the minute hand of the station-clock at Stadtbahnhof Savignyplatz to give us more time. Now, in contrast, I did not want to stop time; I wanted it to accelerate so that Herbert would be safe in the shortest possible time span. I knew that I could be of no help to him now, though my desire to know he was safe was as intense as it was seven months ago. I had entrusted Mr. Höfler with my life, therefore I believed that he would have the same commitment to save Herbert and Lutz. Another hope—or, rather, bit of knowledge—helped to sustain my belief in this night's success: that Herbert's experience as a boy scout and his physical endurance as a former athlete would see him through this night of danger.

Four days later, my suspense ended: Herbert and Lutz had made it! I was told by a young woman in La Ramée, herself an escapee, that she had met Herbert as they had left the prison in Schaffhausen in a little group, to be sent to their different camp destinations. She, scheduled to go to La Ramée, had a little note for me, torn from a newspaper with a few words from Herbert, that he was being sent to a reception camp near Basel; and as a gift from Herbert, she handed me a little book bound in gray linen with Adolph Menzel's drawings, which Herbert had given me in Berlin. It was one of my favorites. Here I was in La Ramée, holding a torn little note and a book of drawings, signifying Herbert's arrival. It was somehow incongruous, and only Herbert could act in such surprising fashion, carrying a briefcase tied around him that contained among a few items this little book, while he crept by night through moonlit meadows across a border, like a soldier under fire. I could have cried from relief that he was saved, and from happiness that he would do such a crazy thing as to bring me a gift under these dangerous circumstances: telling me that he had arrived and that his feelings for me had remained unchanged.

9

Sequelae:
1958; 1983–1990

In 1958, we took our first trip to Germany, after having lived in New York for twelve years. The idea for the trip had come from Herbert, who, during his years of teaching history at the City College of New York, had pursued research about a group of young concentration camp survivors. The postwar atmosphere, especially in New York and in the United States, had been affected immeasurably by what had happened in the concentration camps: General Eisenhower, the war hero and later President, had liberated a camp and had made his abhorrence of what he had seen known to the American public. His report and others that followed, supported by photographs of the dead and dying, had caused disbelief at first, then loathing, which had influenced public thinking in the United States.

At the same time, historians and psychiatrists were writing books, trying to explain the horrors and find out from survivors themselves how they had survived and how they had adjusted to life afterward. Herbert, too, had made contacts with the New School for Social Research, which had been founded by émigré scholars from Germany. With two other researchers, he had done a study of young concentration camp survivors and conducted interviews with them. It was one of the first authentic scholarly statements about that terrible time.

That was the only time, though, that Herbert was professionally involved with the Holocaust. As it was at the Lehranstalt, his research was mainly concerned with the antisemitism that had led to the systematic Nazi persecution and destruction of European Jewry. It was this particular interest that made him use a sabbatical semester to do research on the topic at one of Germany's universities. The university of his choice was Heidelberg. What he was looking for in the university library and its archives was what he called "Social Darwinism before Darwin-ism." While he was writing his dissertation in Bern in 1945, he found that political thinking in Germany before Darwin had already been influenced by the materialism of nineteenth-century science which had undermined the belief that man acted morally and that society had a moral basis. Herbert believed that ideas like these were at the bottom of racism: man was an animal. He chose the University of Heidelberg for its library resources and wanted to spend a good part of his sabbatical semester tracing this idea.

Herbert also chose Heidelberg for practical reasons. Heidelberg was the headquarters of the U.S. army in Germany. It was called USAREUR, and attached to it was an elementary school for army dependents. We made sure that you, Janie, could attend the school. In our planning of this trip you played an important part, because we tried to combine several purposes. First, there was Herbert's research, but we also planned a quasi-reunion with our families. We wanted to see Ludwig and Ilse again and to introduce you to them. I still remember fondly how you and Ludwig walked hand in hand—for one fleeting moment grandfather and granddaughter. And my brother, Helmut, and his wife, and Edith, Herbert's sister, were coming from Israel to meet us in Europe. We wished to make our dispersed family a living new cell, for your sake. I also wanted to show you Wolfenbüttel.

Since the time I had left Wolfenbüttel in 1932, my parental home had undergone some changes. Before my parents left, in 1937, my mother had divided a large apartment into two smaller ones and rented one to our Jewish *Religionslehrer*, Mr. Steinberg, who had been given notice by his Christian landlord. The other apartment she had let to a couple whose obligation it was to report to my mother the need for repairs and maintenance for which my parents were responsible.

On November 9, 1938, Kristallnacht, SA men had burned down the synagogue next to our house and had vandalized our apartment. My mother traveled from Berlin to Wolfenbüttel to see what had happened, and when she returned to Kladow, she found it hard to talk about what she had seen in Wolfenbüttel. All she told me was that the sanitation people had to come to remove the heap of broken glass, china, and ruined furniture. The rest she had put in our garage. I understood from what she was saying that the home that she and father had built up during their twenty-six years of married life, where my brother and I had grown up, had been wrecked—violently, intentionally destroyed—and my mother was too wretched to speak about it.

In 1958, when we arrived by boat from New York in Rotterdam, we had planned to pass through Wolfenbüttel as one of our first stops. I knew that I would not find anything that would remind me of our life in our former house in the Lessingstrasse, but I wanted to show Herbert and you where I had spent my childhood. I also wanted to say hello to the caretaker couple and, especially, to our tenant, Mrs. Baars.

Entering the caretaker's apartment, I realized immediately that some of our furniture stood in their entranceway. When we were asked into the living room, I became aware in a flash that most of their furniture had been ours: there was the couch with the unmistakable pattern (I could still describe it), the table on which I had done my homework, my father's leather chair, even the little print of Rubens's baby son. I could not walk one step further into that apartment: I felt nauseated, my stomach turned, words failed me: I had to leave, no matter what the others thought. Herbert's eyes followed me in amazement. I left it to him to understand without an explanation. After a few minutes, both of you followed me, and I was able to explain to Herbert more rationally what had occurred.

Though I was upset, I wanted to see Mrs. Baars, who by now was elderly and whom I might not see again. She opened the door for me and called out: "Hänschen, Hänschen," mistaking me for my mother. She was in tears, hugging me, as if she never wanted to let go. When we sat down together, she told me her version of Kristallnacht: the SA men had set the synagogue ablaze and then turned toward our house, not only to vandalize, but also to pull Lehrer Steinberg from his bed and throw him into the flames of the burning synagogue. She had rushed to his help, screaming, trying to restrain them with all the strength she had, finally succeeding. As she told me this story, I could imagine her screaming and screaming and not giving a thought for her own safety. She had suffered a nervous collapse afterward.

As we were sitting together, wrapped up in these events, I felt that it had changed her life and that she would never be free from what had happened. As I looked at her, she appeared to be a very unlikely heroine: she had saved our teacher's life. Later on, after his release from a concentration camp, he was able to leave Germany.

I soon said good-bye to Mrs. Baars. My agitation was so great that I abandoned my plan to visit my favorite teacher, Dr. Kössler. I was eager to get away from Wolfenbüttel and to leave behind me once for all the shadows hovering over my youth and to protect you, Janie, from the worst.

This European trip ended with a small adventure for you that we all enjoyed hugely. We had driven to Schaffhausen to show you "our prison." When we came across a motorcycle-policeman, we flagged him down and asked for directions. He was taken aback for the moment but caught himself fast: "Were you in there before?" When we answered in the affirmative, he said with a broad grin: "Well, you are in good company; a short time ago, the President of the Hamburg Senate yielded to the same urge. I shall escort you on my motorcycle and show you the way." Thus, we had an "official escort" guiding us through town until we reached the prison. You felt it a great honor and through the open roof of our Volkswagen observed every inch of the way with great excitement.

When introduced, we were received in a friendly way by the policeman on duty in the prison, but Mr. Brütsch-Mäder had retired and was no longer there. His colleagues called him at home, and he said he would be glad to see us. Another motorcycle escort guided us to his house. It was a touching and cordial reunion, as he saw with his own eyes that the *Liebschaft* of fifteen years earlier had grown into a well-settled small family. We all enjoyed the visit, a gesture of our gratitude for his upright sympathy in our hours of distress. We all lined up in front of Mr. Brütsch-Mäder's garden fence to create a photographic memento of our cordiality and of this rare occasion.

In 1982, a peculiar coincidence in Herbert's professional life led us back once again to Germany for a more prolonged and serious meeting with the past. Herbert had been involved for about eight years in initiating the research and directing the compiling of a four-volume *International Biographical Dictionary of Central European Émigrés, 1933–1945* of the Nazi period. He had set up a team in New York at the Research Foundation for Jewish Immigration and cooperated with the Institut für Zeitgeschichte in Munich in what became a large and time-consuming project. It brought him together with colleagues in Germany, some of whom, like Manfred Briegel in Bonn and the people in Munich, became good friends of his.

The dictionary demonstrated in a concentrated way the great loss sustained by German culture, when the Nazis had dismissed Jewish and politically undesirable scholars, artists, and community leaders from all positions in 1933. With its ten thousand names, it showed clearly that German Wissenschaft had migrated with the émigrés and that many had become extremely creative in the many countries that had taken them in.

Because of his work on the *Dictionary*, Herbert had become known in Germany as an expert on antisemitism and Jewish migrations during the Nazi period. As a result, he was approached by the Technische Universität in Berlin to found and direct a new Zentrum für Antisemitismusforschung (Center for Antisemitism Research). The suggestion to him was a "do-or-die" proposition: no Herbert = no Zentrum. The kind of institute they had in mind would be unique to Germany, even to Europe, and it was clear to Herbert that it would be an unusual challenge to him to take up this idea and bring it to life in historic and scholarly ways. He was well versed in American research in the subject, and wanted to adapt his special knowledge to Germany—the émigré bringing knowledge back to his country of origin. It was a kind of reverse process.

It was a difficult decision to go to Berlin for an uncertain time, given our history in Germany, and to separate from our young family—you, Janie, had already married, and we now had two granddaughters, Madeline, ten, and Leslie, seven. In a telephone conversation, involving Herbert in Berlin and you, Janie, and me at your home in Pennsylvania, we decided to accept the proposition to go to Berlin for three years. For me Berlin held two kinds of memories: my parents and my friends had been murdered, I had almost been killed by Nazi persecution, but we had survived with the help of Germans who had risked much in extending this aid. I went with considerable hesitation.

It was slightly ironic that one of the first conferences dealing with the persecution and emigration we both attended in Germany was held in, of all places, Wolfenbüttel. It had been selected because its library had become world-famous among postwar scholars for its unique resources on European cultural history since the Renaissance.

In 1983, it had been fifty years since Nazi tyranny had led to the dismissal of Jewish teachers and scholars from German universities and scholarly institutes. This three-day conference, set up by the Gesellschaft für Wissenschaftsgeschichte, the German Society for the History of Scholarship, was held in commemoration of that event. Herbert's *Dictionary* had appeared in time to give substance to the commemoration of these losses, and he was invited to attend as an honored guest and to listen to papers about the different disciplines and their losses. I had received an invitation to accompany him on this occasion.

By coincidence, neither Herbert nor I were unknown to the German public at the time because the Bavarian Film Studio had made a TV film depicting our escape. The original English version had been aired at the New York Film Festival in 1981; a German translation had been televised shortly before our arrival. The English title was "We were German Jews"; the German title, "Herbert Strauss, Flüchtling." As a result, the members of the conference knew who I was and that they were meeting in my former hometown. Everybody wished to create a warm atmosphere. But the problem was I had to contend with my memories.

As always on my visits, I saw to it that my grandfather's, uncle's, and aunt's graves were properly cared for. My uncle and aunt's children cared for the graves the same way, but they did not visit Wolfenbüttel as often as I. I had been as close to Uncle Nathan and Aunt Lene as their own children, who had left Germany early.

Nathan and Lene Schloss had an especially tragic fate. On November 9, 1938, Kristallnacht, when the synagogue was burned down and our house vandalized, a horde of SA men entered their house in Halchterstrasse at night, made shambles of their furnishings, pulled them out of bed, and proceeded with violent force to arrest Uncle Nathan. When Lene cried out, they silenced her by beating her with a truncheon across her face. Her nose was broken, and her face disfigured. After these terrible events, she was without help: her husband had been taken to a concentration camp, their daughters had emigrated and my parents, her brother and sister-in-law, had moved to Kladow. She went into a deep depression that she could not overcome.

During the summer of 1939, after Nathan was released from the concentration camp, they came to Kladow for a visit. She was distraught and spent long hours in the garden by herself, as if being alone in nature could still her fears. When Uncle Nathan insisted on returning to Wolfenbüttel to fulfill his obligations as president of the congregation, she went back with him and committed suicide not long afterward, in September 1939. Nathan died of a heart attack in January 1942. He had been forced to arrange for the deportation of the congregation. On the day the transport was to leave for the East, he died on the station platform.

My parents' house was across the street from the main building of the library. I had walked innumerable times along its park and the armory on my way to school in the *Schloss* (castle). When we were invited by the director of the library, Dr. Paul Raabe and his wife, for tea in his garden, we sat in full view of my parents' former house. The reception the *Bürgermeister* gave for the members of the conference was held in the rooms of my former school, the *Schloßschule* restored to their ducal splendor. It seemed incongruous to me that I would be welcomed as a former citizen of Wolfenbüttel while painful memories crowded in on me. Much as I understood the good intention of the public acclaim, I missed any mention of the horrible events that had destroyed my family and my community. In fact, a written history of the town of Wolfenbüttel, published by the city government, which I received as a present at the reception, makes no mention of the Jewish community there, its contribution to town life, and its tragic end.

Some grating overtones were also part of a meeting with Ursula Wrede, a former classmate of mine who wanted to see me. She told me of her war experiences as a secretary, having been

attached to Generalfeldmarschall von Kesselring's army when it
was stationed near Warsaw at the time of the Warsaw ghetto
uprising. For her, it was an unforgettable event. When they
learned what was going on and could not do anything but listen
to the noise, the shooting day and night, and then watch the
flames rising from the ghetto, she said, "in order not to listen,
not to see, not to know, the only thing left to us was to drink
ourselves into oblivion, and that was exactly what we did!"

We also made a pleasant new contact. We received an invitation from Professor Walter Killy, director of research at the library, to visit him and his wife in their home in Salzdahlum, a
village near Wolfenbüttel and well known to me since childhood. My image was of an old North German peasant hamlet,
huddled around a medieval stone church. Red brick farmsteads,
the building year, and the names of the owners cut into wooden
beams across the entrance, barns and courtyards with piles of
manure—all belonged to my memory of Salzdahlum. The cobblestone street unevenly weaving through the village was part
of it, too. But nothing of this image of mine materialized, as we
approached the old village. Sixty years had passed since I had
seen it; it was not surprising that it had changed. We saw modern ranch-style houses with large picture windows overlooking
a garden settlement. In one of the pleasant-looking houses, we
found Professor and Mrs. Killy.

We were welcomed by them with a special warmth and soon
a lively conversation ensued. It seemed to me that we shared
many opinions and felt a special affinity for each other. Their
lives and their fate, as we learned, were very unusual. Mrs. Killy
was of Jewish descent: her father had been a Social Democratic
official of the Prussian government and had to flee for his life in
1933. As a child, she was smuggled out of Germany and was
reunited with her father in the United States, where she was
raised and educated.

Walter Killy had been a soldier in the German army during
the war, became a prisoner of war in a U.S. POW Camp, and
was recognized there as a potential leader in the future German
democracy, for which the United States was trying to prepare
the conditions. He was sent to the United States to study at a
university there and selected as his major German literature. It

was there that he met his future wife. After the war, he became a leading scholar in German literature, and he fulfilled the role of educator he had taken on as an American POW.

To our surprise, our relationship cooled quickly when they realized that we understood our relationship to Germany as different from theirs. Our behavior and our language was familiar to them, but the drastic change that had taken place in us they could not see or understand. We had lived for nearly forty years in America. It had changed us. When I saw New York for the first time, I thought that the city would explode any minute with so many different kinds of people living here together. How we found a place to live in this multitude, how we made a living is a separate tale to tell. My interests had changed, too. I saw people differently. As time went on, I could not imagine returning to my old environment and calling it home. I had become an American or, better, a New Yorker.

In Wolfenbüttel, the conference went well: Herbert was asked to introduce his ideas about emigration and given the go-ahead to describe what happened to migrants moving from one country to another, and if these migrants were scholars and artists, what happened to their scholarship and art. What he saw was not merely "exile." On the contrary. Scholars and artists continued to be creative and often felt enriched by relating to the culture of their new homeland. Those among the émigrés who had strength responded to the challenge and accepted new cultural stimuli, combining the old with the new. Herbert saw this combination as the core of the acculturation process. It was our experience, too, and he had recognized it as being universal. These émigrés succeeded in building up creative and useful lives in their disciplines and thus carried a sense of victory over Nazism.

Herbert's formulations on this topic were received with enthusiasm. The scholars at the meeting even went a step further and charged Herbert to direct a project on this very subject.

What happened at the conference and at the Zentrum für Antisemitismsforschung was not something that concerned only Herbert and his work: what he did was of vital concern to me. He had promised me that he would see to it that I could follow the building of the Zentrum stone by little stone, so that I could see the mosaic of the whole building he was to construct and see it grow. After all, that was why we had come to Berlin.

As Herbert approached the task, it was exciting to see how much support he received from the people at the Technische Universität, especially from the then Chancellor Michael Höbich, and how many young people were interested in the topic and wanted to work with him. For each position at the center, many young people applied; it was a sign of the widespread interest found among German students at the time to explore their past and ours. As they worked at the center, they became closer to us and formed a community that made me feel included. They, Herbert's colleagues and co-workers, especially his secretary, Ingeborg Medaris, gave us a new and different outlook on the attitudes and the goodwill we found again in Berlin.

As it turned out, we stayed longer than the three years we had planned to—they stretched to eight years of exciting personal and intellectual life. Herbert shared with me his contacts in the different circles of his professional life, although we did suffer periods of discomfort and unease as the past would re-emerge in our minds in those familiar streets. He saw his discomfort as part of his professional challenge and gained recognition for his effort to help people understand this great breakdown of human decency in German history. We moved in an atmosphere of like-minded people. Even if antisemitism had not yet fully disappeared, it was almost as if we now witnessed another Germany. We joined the Jüdische Gemeinde, went to religious services and cultural affairs, and Herbert was asked frequently to speak about his work in Berlin and elsewhere.

To me it was a great relief that West Berlin still had Allied military contingents as *Schutzmächte*, protective powers, for its precarious location in the midst of Communist East Germany. We were offered the sociability of the American diplomatic colony and were frequent guests at dinner parties and on national holidays: Berlin was the only place where we ever attended a Fourth of July military parade. I joined the German-American Women's Club and made many new friends among the American and German women of the club.

This, of course, is another story, but when we left Berlin in 1990 and returned to New York after eight years—interrupted by frequent visits to Yardley, to Israel, and to New York—we left many good friends and colleagues behind. Both Herbert and I felt that the spirit that had guided the few Germans who had helped us to survive was alive in the community that had crystallized around our work now for a better present and future. We hoped it would become the standard by which human relations would be measured, as new generations grow into their responsibilities.

EPILOGUE

July 20, 1999

Dear Janie,

The "letter" I had started twenty years ago was not completed until recently—and now it has become a book. The times we survived exercised their own will! "For the Dead *and* the Living we must bear witness." I felt that I should satisfy both of these commands to leave a loving account of my parents and to give you the means to understand what happened to us and to my family; events we tried to keep away from you during your youth should convey to you the coherence we found in ourselves in a most incoherent time.

As a child, you were in Europe, and in the 1980s we showed you, your husband, Bob, and our two granddaughters, Madeline and Leslie, where we had lived in Germany and Switzerland. You knew then that our life, including your upbringing, had won over the terrible past, and it was with satisfaction, even happiness, that we saw that our—your—new family's life was being shaped as it was by our democratic traditions and liberal values. This book will have been worth the pain and effort it took to write if it makes you aware of what binds us together.

YOUR MOTHER